TETON CLASSICS

TETON CLASSICS

50 SELECTED CLIMBS IN
GRAND TETON NATIONAL PARK
SECOND EDITION

RICHARD ROSSITER

FALCON®

GUILFORD, CONNECTICUT
HELENA, MONTANA

AN IMPRINT OF THE GLOBE PEQUOT PRESS

T<small>ETON</small> C<small>LASSICS</small>:
50 S<small>ELECTED</small> C<small>LIMBS</small> <small>IN</small> G<small>RAND</small> T<small>ETON</small> N<small>ATIONAL</small> P<small>ARK</small>, <small>SECOND</small> <small>EDITION</small>

Cover photos by Richard Rossiter. Front Cover: The North Face of the Grand Teton from the summit of Teewinot Mountain. Back Cover: View of the central Tetons. All uncredited photos by the author.
All artwork and graphics are original and by the author.

ISBN 0-934641-71-4

Manufactured in the United States of America
Second edition/Second printing

On the second pitch of Prospector Falls, Death Canyon

Acknowledgments

THE INFORMATION IN this book is derived from my personal experience in the Tetons and from the knowledge and experience of friends and associates. For providing route descriptions, first ascent data, photographs, and general expertise, I would like to thank Gene Ellis, Paul Gagner, Tim Hogan, Ted Kerasote, George Meyers, and Jack Tackle. The Teton ranger staff including Jim Springer, Susan Harrington, and Mark Magnuson were very helpful as were Micheal Keating and Rex Hong of Teton Mountaineering.

Table of Contents

South Buttress Right, pitch three, Mount Moran

Introduction

AMONG THE DISTINGUISHING CHARACTERISTICS of the Teton Range is that, from the east, it rises very abruptly, without the typical intermediary of foothills. The lower slopes of the range, cloaked in trees and jewel-like lakes, simply fall away beneath several thousand feet of sheer rock, glaciers, and hanging snowfields that stand in stark contrast to the arid, sage-dotted plains of Jackson Hole. The highest peak in the range, the Grand Teton, soars 7000 feet above the floor of a valley that was once the haunt of Indians and mountain men. Most of the summits are fairly narrow with all the highest peaks lined up along the western margin of the flat valley. The ultimate effect is that of a great, impregnable wall like the Ered Nimrais in J.R.R. Tolkein's trilogy, the Lord of the Rings. Though there are other very dramatic mountain ranges in this part of the world, such as, the Picket Range in the North Cascades or the Ritter Range in the Sierras, none has the topographical isolation and vertical relief, not to mention ease of access, of the Tetons.

As for climbing, the Tetons offer a wide range of compelling options in an incomparable alpine setting. The routes vary from enjoyable scrambles such as the East Face of Teewinot, to high angle rock masterpieces like the South Buttress Right on Mount Moran. There are the great alpine classics such as the Black Ice Couloir on the Grand Teton and sweeping snow climbs like the Glacier Route on the Middle Teton. During winter, even the easiest routes become challenging and one can expect deep snow, verglace, high winds, and extreme cold. The Owen-Spalding route on the Grand Teton is the most frequented winter climb. Several waterfalls form up, such as Prospector Falls and Rimrock Falls in Death Canyon and provide excellent, steep ice climbs.

Teton rock is generally quite solid and for the most part has good cracks. Contrary to popular notion, the peaks do not consist entirely of granite. Precambrian gneiss and schist form the core of the range with only the highest peaks from Buck Mountain to Leigh Canyon having a preponderance of granite, and even within the granite there are large, angular masses of the more ancient gneiss. Thus, on a single climb one usually will encounter more than one type of rock. Further, a labyrinth of granite and pegmatite dikes runs throughout the range with massive, vertical dikes of black diabase distinguishing several of the main peaks. Teton rock provides excellent climbing with abundant holds and reasonable protection. In the case of incipient cracks or blank areas where nuts can not be placed, one may find fixed pins and the occasional bolt.

On Equipment

In the Tetons, appropriate climbing hardware can vary drastically from one route to another, and for any, what a climber chooses to bring is clearly a matter of taste and style. With this in mind, it is almost ridiculous to make suggestions. But for whatever assistance it may give, the following gear likely would prove adequate on most Teton climbs:

- RPs #2, 3, 4, and 5
- Wired stoppers up to one inch
- 3 or 4 TCUs
- 2 or 3 Hex nuts or Tri-cams
- Various camming devices up to three inches (#4 Friend)
- 6 or 7 quick draws
- 5 or 6 runners long enough to wear over the shoulder
- 7 or 8 unoccupied carabiners (typically with the runners)

Snow and ice climbs such as the Black Ice Couloir typically will require crampons, ice axe(s), snow pickets or flukes, and ice screws as well as some part of the rock climbing gear listed above and a selection of pitons. Specific equipment suggestions are given with most route descriptions.

Note. That certain equipment brand names are sometimes given is not to express a prejudice against others but because certain brands have been long in common use, they serve as a standard of measurement. For example, it is easier to describe the maximum width of a crack in terms of a #3 Friend than inches simply because a climber is more likely to carry a #3 Friend than a ruler. I am NOT suggesting that the named device is in any way superior to similar devices of a different manufacture.

Ratings

The system used for rating difficulty in this book is simply a streamlined version of the so-called Yosemite Decimal System. Which is to say that the class five designation is assumed and that 5.0 through 5.14 is written as 0 through 14 without the 5. prefix. The Welzenbach classes 2 through 4 have been retained and appear in the text as cl2, cl3, and cl4. The Roman numerals I through VI for overall difficulty also are employed in the usual manner. No symbols are used to designate the relative safety of a climb.

At best, any rating represents a consensus of opinion from some of the climbers who have completed a route; it is still opinion and nothing more. People have debated the difficulty of climbs since the sport began and no doubt will continue to do so. Please remember that this book is only a guide to the routes; in the end, it is your skill and good judgment that will keep you alive on the rocks.

The Snaz, seventh pitch, Death Canyon

Environmental Considerations

It goes without saying that the magnificent landscape and fragile ecosystem of the Tetons is a precious heritage and that it deserves our deepest respect, appreciation, and best effort toward preservation. Unlike parks in a more urban setting where disposable diapers, food containers, and Kleenex lurk behind every bush, the Tetons are refreshingly clean and well-kept; relatively conscious and well educated visitors and vigilant park staff are likely the significant factors. As for the sport of climbing, perhaps the greatest environmental impact is from off-trail foot traffic. There is the occasional food wrapper, bit of tape, and toilet paper showing from under rocks - even cigarette butts stuffed into cracks - but it is the long term wear and tear of feet, especially clad in mountain boots, that leave a lasting scar in the mountains.

To preserve the natural beauty and ecological integrity of our climbing environment, a few suggestions are offered. Deposit solid human waste away from camps and paths of approach. Do not cover it with a rock, but leave it exposed to the elements where it will deteriorate more quickly. In the lower forests it can be buried. Carry used toilet paper out in a plastic bag or wipe with a stick or Douglas fir cone. Do not leave man-made riff-raff lying about. If you pack it in, pack it out. Take care to preserve trees and other plants on approaches and climbs. Use trails and footpaths where they have been developed, and demonstrate human evolution by removing obstructions, stacking loose rocks along the trail sides, and picking up trash. When hiking across tundra, follow footpaths or step on rocks to avoid crushing the fragile plantlife.

Fires are allowed only at campsites with firegrates. It is best to use portable campstoves for all cooking. Do not feed or interfere with birds and animals. Bears are natural scavengers; they will tear into and eat anything that smells remotely like food. It is essential to hang food 10 feet or more above the ground. Some campsites have metal poles with hooks for this purpose. In other cases, food should be slung from tree limbs so that it is six feet from the tree and ten to twelve feet off the ground. Check with the National Park Service for other suggestions and regulations.

Weather and Snow Conditions

Climbing in the Tetons is done primarily from mid June through September. During this period one can expect comfortable to hot daytime temperatures, sunny mornings, and afternoon thundershowers. Up until mid July, nearly every peak climb will require an ice axe and mountain boots for some part of the approach, climb, or descent. From late July through August, the weather is usually hot during the day and many climbs can be done without any snow travel. There is typically an auspicious period of two or three weeks in late July or August distinguished by a lack of afternoon thunderstorms. Temperatures will cool some in September but the climbs are usually still dry. By October the first serious snows may come but good climbing can still be had, especially on south-facing features. In November, it gets cold and the winter ice climbs begin to form up. Spring is avalanche time in the Tetons. Check with the rangers for conditions.

Visitor Facilities and Services

Though there is a campground and visitor center at Colter Bay, climbers primarily will be interested in the visitor center at Moose and the rustic ranger station at Jenny Lake (telephone: (307) 733-2880). The rangers who work at this location all are experienced Teton climbers and have a wealth of practical information for the asking. Guide books and maps are available at either facility.

Nearly all climbing activity begins and ends at the Jenny Lake ranger station, not only for its strategic proximity to the main peaks, but because the National Park Service requires climbers to register in person for every outing. One also must check-in upon return. Note that this regulation may be eliminated by the summer of 1994 so that registration will be voluntary as it is in most other national parks. A back country permit, however, still will be required for overnight outings. New regulations regarding rescue insurance also are being considered so that the cost of a rescue is borne by the climber rather than the tax payer. It is just and wise that we take responsibility for our own actions in the mountains as in all facets of our lives. When we ask the government to pay, we invite regulation, higher taxes, and loss of freedom.

Highway 191 is the main road going north from the town of Jackson, Wyoming. To reach Moose and Jenny Lake from Highway 191, turn west at Moose Junction onto the Teton Park Road. The first turn on the right leads to Dornan's where one finds a climbing shop (mountain bike rental), grocery store (canoe rental), liquor store, bar/lounge, gas station, and other conveniences. Continuing west on the Teton Park Road, encounter the Moose Visitor Center on the right and Moose Village stores on the left (with post office). Next, one passes through an entrance station where a fee is required. Pick up a park map (no extra charge) and a copy of Teewinot, a park tabloid with much useful information.

Follow the road as it bends around to head north and after seven super-scenic miles turn left at South Jenny Lake Junction. Another quarter-mile or so brings one to the Jenny Lake complex. The most strategic campground for climbers is at Jenny Lake. See also Gros Ventre and Signal Mountain Campgrounds. There are many other facilities inside the park and in the town of Jackson including good restaurants, laundromats, outdoor shops, and way too much to list here. Stop at the Jackson Chamber of Commerce for a map of town and list of services.

The Climber's Ranch, operated by the American Alpine Club, is located four miles north of Moose on the west side of the Teton Park Road. The Ranch offers overnight accommodations and showers at very reasonable rates. A bunk in a cabin (with four to eight bunks) and communal shower go for $5.00 per night. Bring your own sleeping bag and cook gear. The Ranch also has a library. Of course, if one is accustomed to black tie room service and five star dining....

Write or call:
The Climber's Ranch
P.O. Box 57
Moose, WY 83012
(307) 733-2271

Limitations of Book

This book is intended for the experienced climber; it is not a manual of instruction, but a guide to the routes. It assumes that the reader is already proficient in the placement of climbing hardware, the use of a rope, and has climbed before in the mountains. At least two climbing schools are available in the park for those who seek instruction or the service of a guide. Whereas this book contains much useful information, it cannot take the place of skill and good judgment. Take care in planning an ascent. Be sure to have proper gear and clothing. Allow adequate time to complete the route; an unplanned bivouac can be disastrous. Teton weather can deteriorate rapidly, and a bright, sunny day can turn into a violent storm. Rockfall can occur on any route at any time. Regardless of experience, if the situation in which you find yourself does not look good, consider retreat. You can always return another day.

Topo Symbols

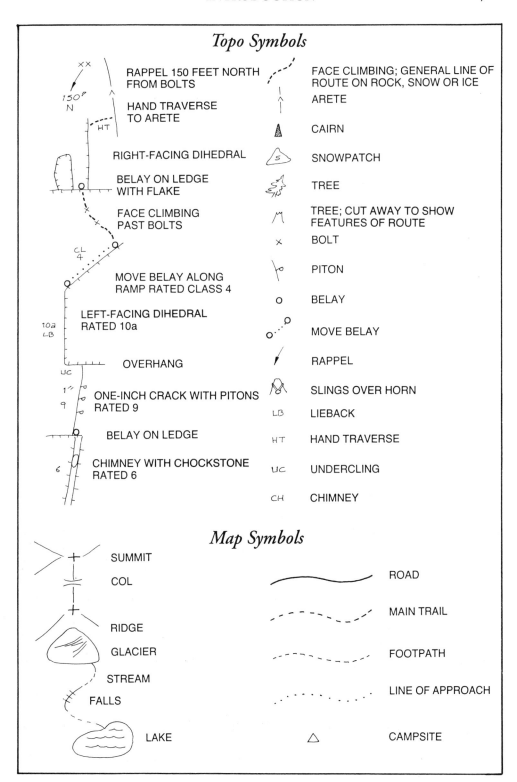

RAPPEL 150 FEET NORTH FROM BOLTS

HAND TRAVERSE TO ARETE

RIGHT-FACING DIHEDRAL

BELAY ON LEDGE WITH FLAKE

FACE CLIMBING PAST BOLTS

MOVE BELAY ALONG RAMP RATED CLASS 4

LEFT-FACING DIHEDRAL RATED 10a

OVERHANG

ONE-INCH CRACK WITH PITONS RATED 9

BELAY ON LEDGE

CHIMNEY WITH CHOCKSTONE RATED 6

FACE CLIMBING; GENERAL LINE OF ROUTE ON ROCK, SNOW OR ICE

ARETE

CAIRN

SNOWPATCH

TREE

TREE; CUT AWAY TO SHOW FEATURES OF ROUTE

BOLT

PITON

BELAY

MOVE BELAY

RAPPEL

SLINGS OVER HORN

LIEBACK

HAND TRAVERSE

UNDERCLING

CHIMNEY

Map Symbols

SUMMIT

COL

RIDGE

GLACIER

STREAM

FALLS

LAKE

ROAD

MAIN TRAIL

FOOTPATH

LINE OF APPROACH

CAMPSITE

Cathedral Rock

Death Canyon

DEATH CANYON IS the second major drainage north from the southern margin of Grand Teton National Park. This deep, glacier-carved valley is one of the most popular approaches to the Teton Crest Trail and, along with great hiking, presents some of the best crag climbing in the range. The main attraction during summer is Cathedral Rock, the 1000-foot southwest buttress of Point 10552. During winter, the canyon provides a fine ski tour and several excellent ice climbs.

To reach Death Canyon from Moose Junction, drive south on the Moose-Wilson Road. After several miles, turn right at a signed junction and drive about 0.7 mile to where a right branch goes to White Grass Ranch (now closed). Bear left and continue for about a mile to a parking area at White Grass Ranger Station and the end of the road. During winter, this road is not plowed.

The Death Canyon Trail begins at the end of the road. It climbs gently for about 1.4 miles to a scenic shoulder above Phelps Lake, then descends across a talus slope into the narrows of Death Canyon. The Sentinel Turret appears up the canyon as the steep tower on the north side. After a level stretch in the forested valley bottom, two switchbacks place the trail higher on the north slope. A long level section passes beneath Omega Buttress, Sentinel Gully, and the Sentinel Turret, the trail then climbs more steeply via six switchbacks directly beneath Cathedral Rock. A footpath

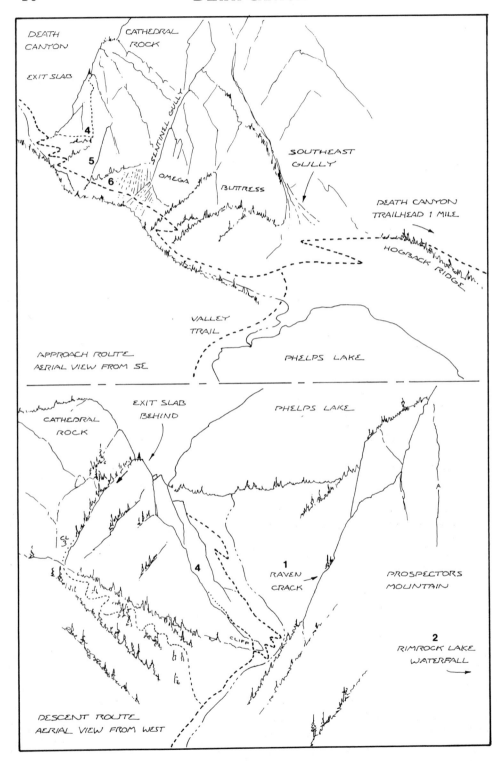

APPROACH ROUTE
AERIAL VIEW FROM SE

DESCENT ROUTE
AERIAL VIEW FROM WEST

that leads to the beginning of the routes on Cathedral Rock climbs back to the northeast from the last switchback. The main trail levels off a short way beyond this point and at 2.5 miles from the trailhead reaches a patrol cabin and a junction with the Alaska Basin Trail. West of here, the canyon opens up and the trail climbs gently for a couple of miles. A final series of switchbacks leads to Fox Creek Pass and a junction with the Teton Crest Trail.

Winter Ice Climbs on Prospectors Mountain

Prospectors Mountain (11241) rises to the west of Phelps Lake and forms the south side of Death Canyon. It holds several alpine tarns and has a very rugged northeast face across Death Canyon from Cathedral Rock and Omega Buttress (see below).

1. Prospector Falls
IV WI4

Also known as Raven Crack Falls, this is the large ice formation on the northeast face of Prospectors Mountain across Death Canyon from the Sentinel Turret. The climb consists of four pitches of ice with the second and fourth pitches being the most difficult. Some parties complete only the first two pitches. By November or December, when the ice is well-formed, skis or snowshoes are needed for the approach. The route first was climbed by Dave and Peter Carmen during the early 1970s. The Nugget (WI4+) is a steep smear up the big couloir immediately west of Raven Crack Falls. Beware of avalanche.

Approach. Follow the Death Canyon Trail until it comes near to the stream below Cathedral Rock, then cross the drainage and ski south to the bottom of the falls.

The Route.

1. Climb a 50-foot bulge and belay on an ice ledge.

2. Tackle the 150-foot vertical section and belay where the angle eases back.

3. Do an easy pitch up to the left, then curve back right and belay at the base of the final steep section.

4. Climb 100 feet of steep ice to a large bench. Make five long rappels from trees to the west of the falls.

2. Rimrock Falls
IV WI4

Rimrock Lake is a secluded tarn high on the north face of Prospectors Mountain about 2000 feet above the Death Canyon Trail. The cascade that descends northward from the lake provides about 900 feet of ice climbing in three sections of ascending difficulty. The first ascent was made on 20 February 1977 by Richard Rossiter and Jeff Splittgerber. The ice is best during mid to late winter. Skis or snowshoes are needed for the approach.

Approach. Hike (ski) the Death Canyon Trail to a point about one mile beyond Cathedral Rock where the trail crosses to the left side of the main stream. Rimrock Falls will be seen directly to the south. The first section of ice is about 300 yards south of the trail.

The Route.

    I. Climb about 175 feet of variable ice up to 55 degrees, then slog 300 feet of snow and/or slabby ice.

    II. Do three long leads over ice slabs and bulges up to 60 degrees. Climb about 500 feet of snow with some ice bulges and belay at the base of the final steep section.

    III. Climb two magnificent pitches of bluegreen ice from 70 to 90 degrees and arrive in the hanging cirque of Rimrock Lake.

Descent. Slog down the broad gully to the west of the upper formation, then follow the main couloir until it again steepens. Traverse northeast and rappel from trees to easy terrain.

Cathedral Rock

Cathedral Rock is the farthest west and most impressive of the major buttresses on the south side of Point 10552. This beautiful feature, more a "wall" than a "rock," looms up dramatically on the north as one hikes through the narrows of Death Canyon. There are several good routes on this very steep wall, two of which - the Snaz and Caveat Emptor - have become indisputable Teton Classics.

Approach. Hike the Death Canyon Trail to the last of eight switchbacks beneath the southwest corner of Cathedral Wall. Here a steep path cuts back to the right. Climb a short cliff (cl4) and follow the path east to its end beneath the middle of the wall. The cliff at the beginning of this trail is unpleasant to descend, especially if wet and the downclimb does not return to the base of the main wall. Therefore one

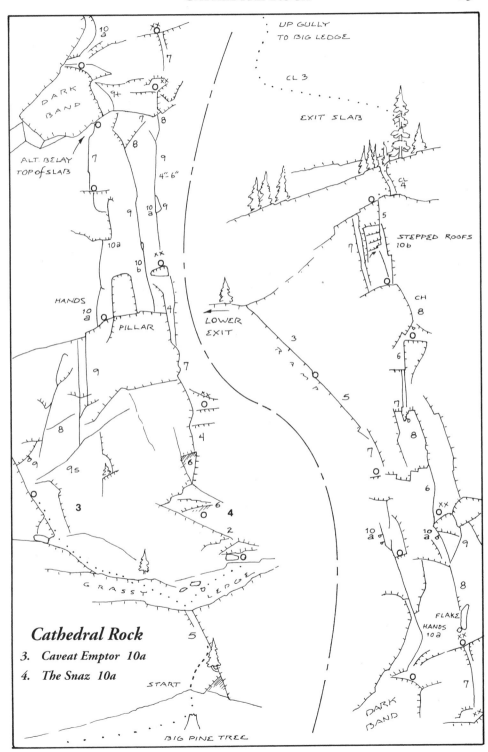

Cathedral Rock

3. **Caveat Emptor 10a**
4. **The Snaz 10a**

may want to stash extraneous gear near the end of the downclimb instead of bringing it up to the beginning of the routes.

For those unfamiliar with Cathedral Rock (as well as those wishing to stash gear), it is a good idea to continue up the main trail to where the southwest side of the cliff can be viewed. The downclimb follows the forested ledge that begins on the right skyline and makes a diagonal down and left across the face to the forest/talus slope. From there, a path leads down through trees and talus to the Death Canyon Trail not far from the patrol cabin.

3. Caveat Emptor
10a

"Let the buyer beware," says the Latin idiom. That the climb deserves such an ominous designation is subject to

Paul Gagner photo

Caveat Emptor, second pitch

question since it is probably the best rock climb in Death Canyon, however, those accustomed to the uncertainty of first ascents may find meaning in the name. It should be mentioned, however, that the last difficult pitch is a bit run out. The line runs parallel on the left and near to The Snaz but is harder and much more sustained in difficulty. The first ascent is credited to Jim Beyer and Buck Tilley who climbed the route as it is described here during July 1979; a number of other people had climbed parts of the route previously. Rack up to 4 inches with extra pieces from one inch up.

The Route.

1. Climb the initial pitch of The Snaz to get up onto the big, grassy ledge (5), then angle up and left on ramps and ledges (4) to the base of a left-leaning chimney.

2. Start up the chimney to a fixed pin, hand traverse right to a crack, and climb straight up (9) to a right-facing corner. Work up the corner, then angle right to belay on a ledge beside a large pillar.

3. To the left of the pillar, climb a beautiful finger crack up to a roof (10a). Turn the roof on the right (10a) and belay on a ledge after about 30 feet. It also is possible to continue up a crack (7) and belay beneath a band of dark rock (165 feet overall).

4. Climb the crack (7) up to an overhang in an area of dark rock (possible belay on slab), make difficult moves up through the roof (10a), and belay across from the detached flake on the sixth pitch of The Snaz (90 feet).

5. Power up through an overhanging handcrack (10a) (possible belay on small ledge), up through a left-facing corner and roof (9), and belay on a ledge that is below and right of some fixed protection (150 feet).

6. Move up and left about 10 feet to a fixed pin, straight up past a bashie (10a), back right to a left-facing corner, and up to a belay ledge (90 feet).

7. Climb an unprotected face (6), then follow a left-angling ramp to a ledge (150 feet).

8. Work up and left along easier terrain to the base of the broad slab above The Snaz.

To descend, climb up and left across the slab to the forested ledge or work straight left. See descent for The Snaz (below).

4. The Snaz
10a

What exactly is a snaz? For an answer, we would have to ask Yvon Chouinard who with Mort Hempel made the first ascent on 4 August 1964. Fine steep rock, a warm southern exposure, and a relatively easy approach and descent combine to make the Snaz one of the most popular pure rock climbs in the Tetons. All of the belays are on good ledges and pitches two through seven have fixed anchors with rappel rings. The protection is good on all pitches including variations. Rack up to 4 inches with extra pieces from one inch up. To find the beginning of the route, hike the climber's path to a large tree beneath an immense open book dihedral that runs up the center of the wall. Step up to the highest ground and belay at a slab beneath a small left-facing corner with a tree.

The Route.

1. Climb up and right into the corner and work up to a broad grassy ledge (5). Run the rope out and belay beneath or just above a blocky overhang (6).

2. Work up a steep, not too clean, left-facing corner, move right and up to a belay at the bottom of another left-facing dihedral (7).

3. Follow the dihedral up through a wide slot and continue up to a good stance beneath an offwidth crack with a wedged block (7).

4. Now the climb gets going. Jam up around the right side of the block (9) and continue up the long, wide crack (8 or 9) to a roof that is turned on the left (8).

5. From the stance above the roof, climb an easy crack and corner to a ledge beneath a large detached flake (7).

6. This is a great pitch. Work up past a loose block and around the left side of the flake, continue up the fist crack (8), then jam and stem out a magnificent overhanging crack to yet another good ledge (10a). It is possible (but not recommended) to avoid the overhang by working around it on the right (9).

7. Work straight up a steep dihedral (7) for about 60 feet, traverse left to the far side of a hanging block (7), then work up through the roof, up short double cracks to a ledge (7), and up a crack on the right to a sloping ledge in an alcove.

8. Make tricky moves up into a bomb bay chimney (8) and follow it until it is possible to step left around an arête to a big ledge.

9. The traditional last pitch takes the double crack and chimney on the left to another ledge (7). For a more climactic but well protected finish, undercling and lieback out the huge, stepped overhang on the right and arrive at the same belay ledge (10b).

Descent. One must go up before going down. Scramble up the chimney above the belay (5) to a ledge with trees. Move right (east) to the largest tree and climb up onto a broad, smooth slab that is slippery when wet. The objective is to reach the higher, forested ledge. Climb straight up the slab to the ledge (cl4) or, more easily, climb up about 60 feet to a small rounded ledge and follow this west for about 300 feet (cl3 or 4, no pro) until it is easy to gain the forested ledge. Once on the ledge, hike west about 400 feet to a three-stone cairn, then descend a gully and chimney system down across the southwest face of Cathedral Rock to the talus (cl3). A series of crude switchbacks (please use them) leads down through the trees to open talus whence a few hundred feet of boulder hopping bring one to the level section of the trail above the eighth switchback. It is possible to royally screw up this descent, especially in the dark. It is, in fact, extremely dangerous to attempt this descent after nightfall. It may be safer to wait until morning when navigational errors can rectified. One also may go straight west from the last belay of The Snaz or Caveat Emptor and descend along a lower series of ledges.

Winter Ice Climbs on Point 10552

Point 10552 is the southern satellite of Static Peak. It would go unnoticed for all eternity except that it forms the very rugged and spectacular north wall at the entrance to Death Canyon. Its prominent features include (from west to east) Cathedral Rock, Sentinel Turret, Sentinel Gully, and Omega Buttress. All ice climbs on this side of the canyon face south into the sun.

5. Sentinel Ice Couloir
III WI4

This climb is not to be confused with the large drainage between Sentinel Turret and Omega Buttress which is called Sentinel Gully. The ice climb ascends the broad couloir on the west side of Sentinel Turret and consists of three or four pitches of ice. Slog up through snow for about 300 feet to reach the ice. A 40-foot pillar on the third pitch is the crux; this can be passed more easily to the left. Rappel from fixed anchors.

6. Dread Fall
III 10a WI5

This transient formation is probably the most difficult ice climb in Death Canyon. It begins directly above the trail about 100 yards west from Sentinel Gully. Bring a selection of ice screws, several LAs and small angles, and #1-3 Friends.

1. Mixed climbing leads up and left through the initial cliff.

2. Climb up and right over thin, low-angle ice (WI3).

3. Climb an ice pillar on the left or a difficult mixed chimney on the right.

4. A final short pitch leads to a ledge (WI3).

To descend, walk west on a ledge and rappel 150 feet from fixed pins and slings around a block to a snow bench. Walk west about 50 yards, then angle down to the trail.

Southeast Gully (I WI2-3). Four or five short ice climbs form above the Death Canyon Trail to the northwest of Phelps Lake (above the Valley Trail junction). The longest of these, the Battle of the Buldge (WI3), is about 150 feet high. These are not Teton Classics but are good warm-up climbs for their big brothers up the canyon.

Aerial panorama of central Teton Peaks from the east

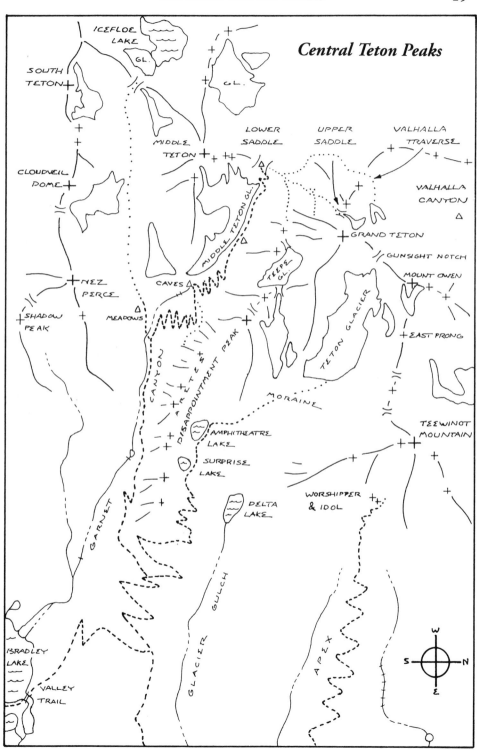

Central Teton Peaks

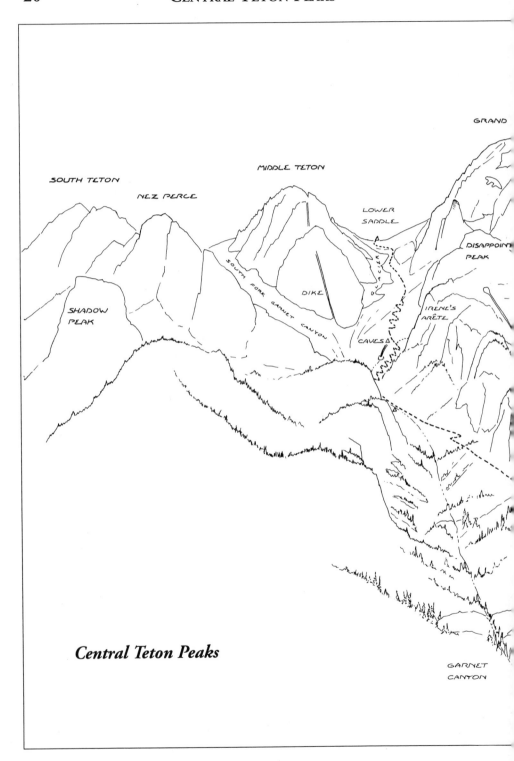

Central Teton Peaks

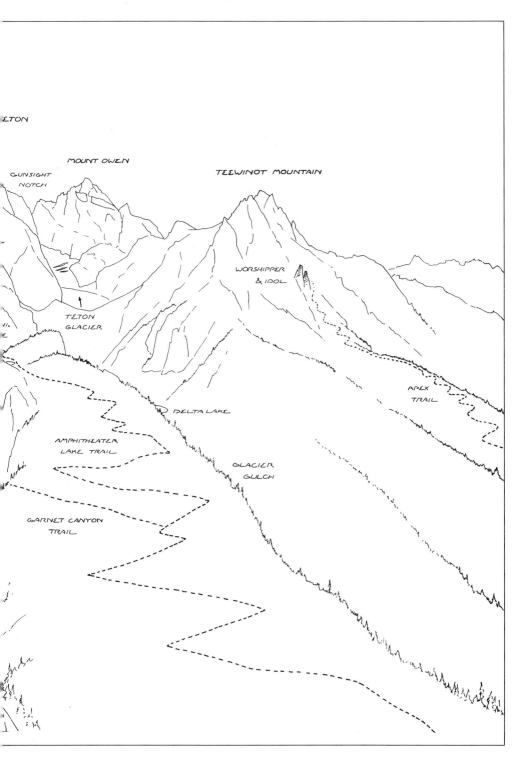

Middle Teton from the north

Middle
Teton

THE MIDDLE TETON (12804) is the third highest peak
in the range. In a more remote location it would no
doubt be less popular but sitting squarely at the head of
Garnet Canyon, immediately adjacent to the busy south
side of the Grand Teton, a certain degree of prestige and
notoriety is guaranteed - and it does present several wor-
thy routes. The Southwest Couloir is one of the more
frequented Teton scrambles while the Middle Teton Glacier and the Northwest Ice
Couloir provide sweeping ascents on classic alpine terrain. The view from the summit is wholly spectacular and yields an excellent reconnaissance of the south ridges
of the Grand Teton. The summit first was reached via the Ellingwood Couloir on
29 August 1923 by Albert Ellingwood, Eleanor Davis, and E. W. Harnden.

Description. Looking south from the Lower Saddle, two pinnacles will be seen
beneath the north ridge: Pinocchio Pinnacle is the nearer, the taller is Bonney's
Pinnacle. Behind, the north ridge climbs directly to the summit, passing en route a
lesser protuberance called the North Peak. Just west of the ridge, the Northwest Ice
Couloir climbs steeply to a notch in the west ridge near the summit. The northwest
face and west ridge are seldom visited by climbers. The unnamed saddle between
the Middle Teton and South Teton (c. 11300) sits to the southwest of the summit
and overlooks Iceflow lake below to the west. Above the saddle, the Southwest
Couloir leads directly to the notch between the north and south summits, the latter
of which is slightly lower.

The rugged south face rises above the South Fork of Garnet Canyon in a series of ridges and gullies including the Ellingwood Couloir which climbs to the col behind the Dike Pinnacle, a summit on the east ridge. The broad east ridge begins just above the Meadows in Garnet Canyon and culminates in the Dike Pinnacle (c. 12400). Beyond the pinnacle, an east-facing headwall sweeps up to the summit. A prominent diabase dike splits the east ridge but veers off to the north of the Dike Pinnacle and traverses the north face to the col behind Bonney's Pinnacle. The Middle Teton Glacier spans the entire north side of the peak from the east ridge to the north ridge and climbs in a narrow phalanx of snow and ice to the col between the Dike Pinnacle and main summit.

Descent. The descent from the summit is the same for all routes: Scramble down the Southwest Couloir route or downclimb and rappel the north ridge to the col behind Bonney's Pinnacle, then reverse the approach to the Northwest Ice Couloir.

7. Southwest Couloir
II Class 3, moderate snow

The Southwest Couloir of the Middle Teton is one of the most popular scrambles in the range. It also is the easiest way to descend from the summit. In early season the couloir yields a fine, moderate snow climb but by August one may expect a long, pleasant hike up talus with a bit of scrambling in the steeper, upper section. An ice axe and mountain boots are recommended for the ascent.

Approach. To reach the bottom of the couloir, take the Garnet Canyon Trail to the Meadows (see under Grand Teton), cross the stream on a narrow wooden bridge, and hike up the South Fork of Garnet Canyon (no distinct trail) all the way to the saddle between the Middle and South Tetons.

The Route. Scramble southeast up the obvious gully to within about 100 feet of the top, move left a bit, and scramble to the north summit. Stretches of snow may be avoided by working up the rock on either side of the couloir. Allow about 5 hours to reach the summit from the Meadows in Garnet Canyon and seven or eight hours from Lupine Meadows. This route was first climbed by H. Oswald Christensen, Morris Christensen, and Irven Christensen, 16 July 1927.

8. Glacier Route
III 4, moderate to steep snow

This classic route ascends the Middle Teton Glacier to the col behind the Dike Pinnacle, then climbs a steep, narrow couloir up the east-facing summit headwall. In early season this is one of the few pure glacier and snow climbs in the Tetons. By mid-season one may expect some moderate rock climbing on the headwall. An ice axe, crampons, and mountain boots are essential as well as a minimal rock climbing rack. Snow flukes or pickets may be useful for belays on the steeper sections and perhaps ice screws should be carried in late season. This route was first climbed on 4 August 1944 by Sterling Hendricks and Paul Bradt.

The Route. Hike the Garnet Canyon Trail to about 10,800 feet where it is obvious to cut south onto the broad apron of the Middle Teton Glacier. Work up and left around the bergschrund and ascend the steep snow gully directly to the col at the west side of the Dike Pinnacle. Now climb a steep, narrow couloir to the notch between the summits or work up slabs and snow patches to the left. The higher north summit is to the right from the notch.

9. Northwest Ice Couloir
III 6, moderately steep ice

The Northwest Couloir is a first class, if moderate, alpine climb and serves as an excellent primer for its big brothers such as the Black Ice Couloir on the Grand Teton. In early season the couloir may be packed with snow and will present little challenge beyond working up a sweat kicking steps. But later, after the seasonal snow has melted off, a fine ice climb is revealed. This hanging couloir lies to the right of the north ridge and finishes at a notch on the west ridge very near to the north summit. The couloir is narrow at the bottom and top and reaches an angle of approximately 50 degrees. Ice screws and a light rock climbing rack are recommended. The first ascent was made by Peter Lev and James Greig on 16 June 1961.

Approach. Hike the Garnet Canyon Trail to the Lower Saddle and head south (see Grand Teton).

The Route. From the Lower Saddle, scramble up to the base of two small rock towers, Pinocchio Pinnacle (the nearer) and Bonney's Pinnacle (the higher of the two). Pass Pinocchio on the west, go through a notch, and pass Bonney's on the east to arrive at a col formed by an eroded diabase dike. Work up to the left, then, back to the right and follow a ledge around into the Northwest Couloir. About 700 feet of snow or ice lead to a notch on the west ridge from which an easy scramble leads to the north summit.

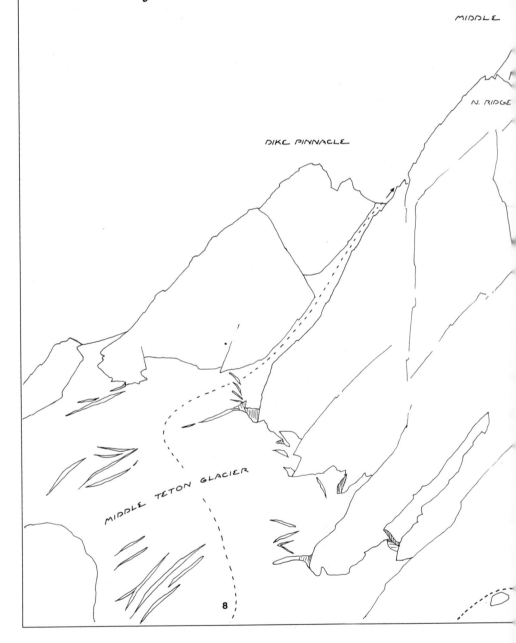

*Middle Teton Overview
viewed from the north*

MIDDLE

N. RIDGE

DIKE PINNACLE

MIDDLE TETON GLACIER

8

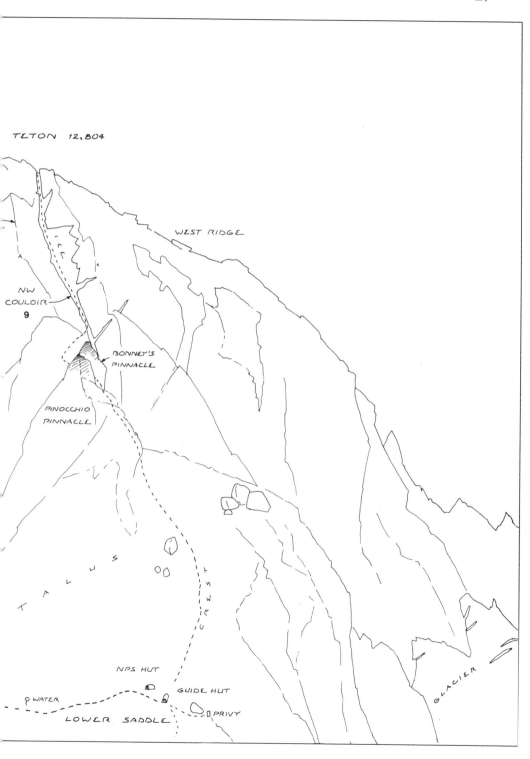

TETON 12,804

WEST RIDGE

NW
COULOIR
9

BONNEY'S
PINNACLE

PINOCCHIO
PINNACLE

T A L U S

CREST

GLACIER

NPS HUT

WATER

GUIDE HUT

PRIVY

LOWER SADDLE

The Grand Teton from the southeast

Grand Teton

A CITADEL OF NAKED ROCK, steep ice gullies, and hanging snowfields, the Grand Teton towers 7000 feet above the valley of Jackson Hole and is, in both image and elevation (13770), the greatest peak of the range. From Jenny Lake the Grand Teton is completely eclipsed by Mount Teewinot but from most other locations in Jackson Hole it is visible and striking. Its powerful, graceful summit stands as the centerpiece in two unique groupings of peaks. From the plains to the east it is seen as the northernmost feature of the skyline trinity, Les Trois Teton, along with the Middle and South Tetons. From the northeast, it is framed in the Cathedral Group with Teewinot and Mount Owen which rise in jagged relief above the mouth of Cascade Canyon.

From a climber's perspective, the broad assortment of excellent routes and the relatively uncomplicated approach by trail (at least to the south side) make the Grand Teton an irresistible objective. It is, not surprisingly, the most popular of the Teton summits. Among its masterpieces are such timeless trade routes as the Owen-Spalding and Exum Ridge and the long, complex alpine imperatives of the North Ridge and the Black Ice Couloir. It is not unreasonable to assert that anyone who fancies himself an alpine climber in America, must sooner or later get acquainted with this outstanding mountain.

The Grand Teton has a rich and complex climbing history, the mere highlights of which are beyond the scope of this presentation, however, the first ascent of the mountain cannot be neglected. Though earlier visits to the summit are claimed by two other parties, the first ascent of the Grand Teton is credited to William Owen, Franklin Spalding, Frank Peterson, and John Shive who reached the summit on 11 August 1898. Their route, now known as the Owen-Spalding, is the most moderate and popular on the peak and is, with rare exception, the only route used to descend from the summit. An excellent history of early climbing is found in *Mountaineering in the Tetons, the Pioneer Period 1898 to 1940*, by Fritiof Fryxell. Also see *A Complete Climber's Guide to the Teton Range* by the late Leigh Ortengburger and Reynold Jackson which, in two volumes, gives historical anecdotes and first ascent information for all known routes in the range.

Description of Peak (counterclockwise). The Lower Saddle (around 11650) is the broad col between the Middle Teton and Grand Teton and is the normal start or finish to nearly every outing on the peak. During the summer one will find here running water, an outdoor toilet, a guide hut, a ranger hut, several stone bivouac enclosures, and... people.

Northeast from the Lower Saddle, a series of gullies and low ridges climbs to the Upper Saddle (c.13160), the col between the Enclosure (around 13320) and the main summit. The Enclosure is the massive west buttress of the Grand Teton which terminates in a secondary summit where a mysterious stone enclosure was discovered in 1872, lending the name. These gullies are bounded on the left by the southwest ridge of the Enclosure and by the Exum Ridge on the right.

The Exum Ridge may be thought of as the true south ridge of the Grand Teton. It is the left of three prominent ridges on the south face of the peak along with the Petzoldt Ridge and the Underhill Ridge (farthest east). Of these, only the Exum Ridge forms a continuous line to the summit. All three ridges rise above a dike of black diabase that cuts across the entire south side of the peak at the 12,160-foot level from the shoulder above the Lower Saddle to the cirque north of Disappointment Peak.

The steep northeast face lies to the north of the Underhill Ridge and is characterized by the Otterbody Snowfield; the Teepe Glacier resides in the cirque below. Teepe Pillar, the familiar guardian of the North Fork of Garnet Canyon, towers above the southwest side of the glacier. Just east of the Teepe Glacier and south of the black dike, are three pinnacles, Pemmican Pinnacle, Fairshare Tower, and the Red Sentinel. A distinct col and couloir separate these towers from the summit of Disappointment Peak (11618).

The longest continuous rampart of the peak is the east ridge which begins between Disappointment Peak and the terminus of the Teton Glacier (c. 10400), then climbs without interruption to the summit. The north side of the ridge drops off abruptly above the Teton Glacier to form the great north face of the Grand Teton.

At the west end of the glacier, a steep ramp, the Grandstand, climbs 1000 feet to form a narrow platform at the bottom of the prominent north ridge. The north ridge is formed by the junction of the upper north and west faces of the Grand Teton.

Valhalla Canyon extends northward from the Grand Teton and drops steeply into Cascade Canyon. It is bounded on the east by the Grandstand and Mount Owen and on the west by the northwest ridge of the Grand Teton (which climbs to the summit of the Enclosure). The headwall of Valhalla Canyon culminates at the Upper Saddle and gives rise to such notable features as the Black Ice Couloir and the Enclosure Couloir. The west side of the Enclosure, at about the 12,000-foot level, is transected by a long ledge system

Paul Gagner photo

North Face of the Grand Teton from the Teton Glacier

that allows passage from the Lower Saddle to routes on the northwest side of the Grand Teton and the Enclosure. This is known as the Valhalla Traverse and brings our tour of the mountain back around to where it began at the Lower Saddle.

Garnet Canyon Trail. By far the most common approach to the Grand Teton is from the east via Garnet Canyon. A fine trail begins from the Lupine Meadow parking area, makes long switchbacks up the forested east slope of Disappointment Peak, contours around into Garnet Canyon, and after seven miles and a 4800-foot elevation gain, terminates at the Lower Saddle (around 11650). The trail above 8960 feet is quite rugged. The final steep headwall immediately below the saddle may be breached directly on snow in early season or via rocks to the right where a heavy rope is normally anchored for a hand rail. The Middle Teton sits dead center at the head of Garnet Canyon and divides its upper reaches into north and south forks. Note that the main trail stays right of the stream at an area called the

Meadows (see below) and follows the North Fork of Garnet Canyon to the Lower Saddle. The South Fork does not have a trail beyond the meadows and terminates at the unnamed col between the Middle and South Tetons.

There are specific areas sanctioned by the Park Service for camping. Several good sites will be found at the Meadows (c. 9300), the beautiful, open area of Garnet Canyon immediately east of the Middle Teton, just before the canyon bifurcates into north and south forks. This is about 4.7 miles from the trailhead and is the lowest of the campsites. At about 5.5 miles and after a series of short, steep switch-backs are the Caves or Petzoldt's Caves (about 10000) which are actually dugouts under huge boulders. Beginning at about 6.2 miles is the Moraine Camp area (about 10800) where one will find a series of stone enclosures or flattened areas along the lateral moraine of the Middle Teton Glacier. The highest and perhaps most strategic campsite is the Lower Saddle (about 11650). Where this scenic perch provides an easier shot at the summit, it is often cold and windy and is seven long, hard miles from the trailhead. Check with the rangers on water, snow conditions, and bear problems when registering for a climb.

Glacier Trail (also known as the Amphitheater Lake Trail). About three miles up the Garnet Canyon Trail, at the last switchback on the east face of Disappointment Peak, a signed trail continues up to the right and after many short switchbacks reaches Surprise and Amphitheater Lakes. From here a climber's path leads north to a small pass from which a rocky ledge with a hand cable allows safe descent into Glacier Gulch. The Teton Glacier lies to the northwest behind the enormous terminal moraine. From here, one has access to routes on the east ridge, north face, and north ridge of the Grand Teton, and to routes on Mount Owen, and Teewinot.

Valhalla Canyon. The third and only other practical approach to the Grand Teton is from the north out of Cascade Canyon. Take the boat across Jenny Lake (or walk the trail 1.6 miles around the south side) and hike about three miles up the Cascade Canyon Trail to a point just west of the drainage from Valhalla Canyon. The north-west side of the Grand Teton is visible from here. Ford Cascade Creek (a log cross-ing may be available) and follow a climber's path up the steep, forested slope to the right of the torrent into Valhalla Canyon. This approach gives access to all routes from the North Ridge to the Enclosure Couloir.

Valhalla Traverse. There is, however, an important alternative for reaching these remote, north-facing routes. The Valhalla Traverse is a long ledge system that, with-out significant obstruction, traverses the entire west side of the Grand Teton and connects the Lower Saddle with upper Valhalla Canyon. Since the only reasonable descent from the summit returns to the Lower Saddle via the Owen-Spalding route, one may, for example, camp at the Lower Saddle, take the Valhalla Traverse, climb the North Ridge, and return to camp without having to carry bivouac gear over the summit; the only way to fly.

Grand Teton viewed from the southwest. The Owen-Spalding ascends the left shadowed area; the Exum Ridge runs down and right from the summit; the next two ridges on the upper mountain are the Petzoldt and Underhill; Glencoe Spire and Teepe Pillar sit down and right from these.

Looking north toward the Grand Teton from the Lower Saddle, identify a cairn on a level section of the southwest ridge that is slightly higher than the Saddle. This cairn marks the beginning of the scree ledge that runs across the west face of the Enclosure. To reach the cairn from the Lower Saddle, hike north on a path about halfway to the Black Dike, cut left and descend into a large scree gully. Cross the gully and make an ascending traverse to the level section of the southwest ridge. When free of snow, a faint trail will be found in this area. Follow the ledge system across the west face to the northwest ridge of the Enclosure and continue around to the north side.

After a short descent (about 20 feet), one must choose an upper or lower version of the traverse. The upper route crosses a bowl (usually on snow or ice) and continues at that level, around into the Enclosure Couloir. This is probably the most common approach to the Black Ice Couloir. The lower route crosses the bottom of the bowl and follows a ramp down into the second icefield of the Black Ice Couloir. This option is used to reach the North Ridge or the original version of the Black Ice Couloir via ramps that diagonal up across the lower west face of the Grand Teton.

South Side

10. Owen-Spalding Route
II 4 to 6

This very popular and important route has the distinction of being the easiest route on the Grand Teton. It is the route by which the peak was first climbed and is almost the only route ever used for descent from the summit. Though it is perhaps less aesthetic than the Exum Ridge and other steeper routes, it has the tactical advantages of being swift and direct, and allows an easy escape in bad weather. A controversy has long existed over the first ascent of this historic route but credit usually is given to Franklin Spalding, William Owen, Frank Peterson, and John Shive who climbed to the summit on 11 August 1898.

Approach. Begin from Lupine Meadow and follow the Garnet Canyon Trail all the way to the Lower Saddle. For the very athletic, the climb may be done "car to car" in one long day. Most folks, however, will want to make a high camp or bivouac and take two or three days for the ascent.

The long, initial section of the Owen-Spalding route is little more than a steep hike which begins from the Lower Saddle and follows a blunt rib up the middle of a wide gully to the Upper Saddle. Though there are several ways to do this part of the climb, one has become standard and requires some description.

The Route. A distinct footpath leads directly up the crest of the saddle from the low point to the black dike. Please use this path and avoid trampling the fragile tundra vegetation.

Above the dike, a prominent rib divides the gully. The first steep tower along this rib is called the Needle. Follow a faint path over rocky terrain to the left (west) of the Needle and continue for several hundred feet to where a short chimney with a chockstone rises to the east. Do not climb the chimney but continue to the north until it is possible to traverse back right over the top of the chockstone and onto a bench at the south side of a large, conspicuous boulder. Now crawl through the tunnel formed by the boulder (the Eye of the Needle) and continue north along a ledge past an exposed move to the gully above the chockstone chimney. This gully is the cut-off point for the Upper Exum Ridge route.

Follow easy ledges and scree (or snow) to an area of black rock. Make a few steep moves up onto the crest of the central rib and continue just on its right side for a couple of hundred feet, then work back into the main gully and scramble for another 300 feet to the Upper Saddle. Or just follow the right edge of the gully all the way.

Note that from winter to early summer the entire route between the black dike and the Upper Saddle may be climbed on snow in the broad gully to the west of the Needle and the central rib.

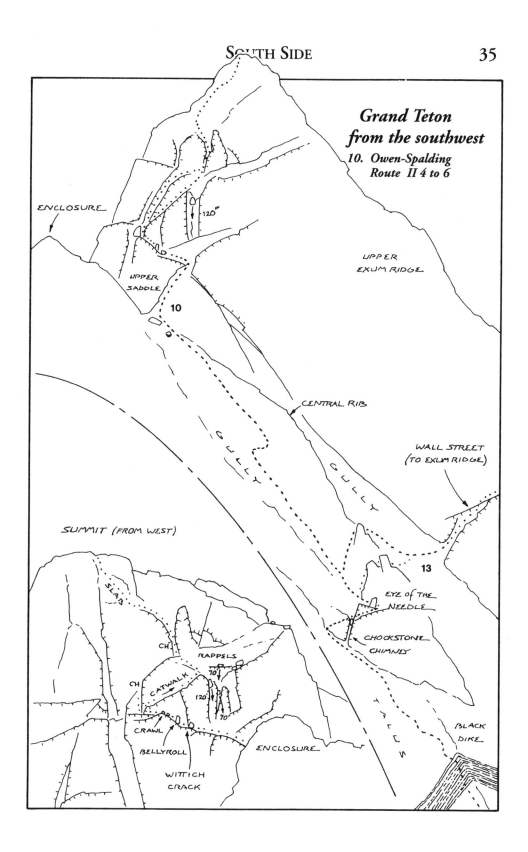

*Grand Teton
from the southwest*
*10. Owen-Spalding
Route II 4 to 6*

ENCLOSURE

120°

UPPER
EXUM RIDGE

UPPER
SADDLE

10

CENTRAL RIB

WALL STREET
(TO EXUM RIDGE)

GULLY

GULLY

13

SUMMIT (FROM WEST)

EYE OF THE
NEEDLE

SLAB

CHOCKSTONE
CHIMNEY

CH

RAPPELS

70'

CATWALK

CH

120°

70'

CRAWL

TALUS

BELLYROLL

ENCLOSURE

BLACK
DIKE

WITTICH
CRACK

From the Upper Saddle, work up and left (east, then, north) along a large scree ledge to where it narrows on the exposed west face of the peak. Pass beneath the steep Wittich Crack and in about 12 feet reach the Belly Roll, a large detached slab that is passed via a hand traverse along its upper edge. In a few more feet one encounters another obstacle known as the Crawl. Crawl through this narrow space or drop down and hand traverse along the edge, then regain the ledge and continue

The Owen-Spalding rappel

about ten feet to a short, overhanging chimney. Climb the chimney (6) or begin with an easier version just around to the left. The two chimneys merge after a very short way. Now a second short chimney brings one to a rubble strewn ledge. This last section is known as the Double Chimney and can be fairly difficult when icy.

Continue upward via the Owen Chimney (see topo page 35) and traverse southeast to the base of yet another chimney that cuts east-northeast through the upper cliff-band. One may avoid the Owen Chimney by scrambling up and right to gain the Catwalk, a long, sloping ramp that leads south to an overlook above the main rappel. This rappel is commonly used on the descent and it is a good idea to verify its location at this time. From the vicinity of a cairn, look for slings around a large block a short way down to the south. From the south end of the Catwalk, scramble northeast up to the chimney in the upper cliffband.

Whether one arrived from the Owen Chimney or the Catwalk, climb the chimney in the upper cliffband for about 50 feet, then branch off to the left in a dihedral. From the dihedral, an easy though slightly indirect scramble leads northeast to the summit.

The Wittich Crack (6) is sometimes less icy than the regular Double Chimney and adds two pitches of excellent rock to the ascent. Begin at the obvious vertical crack system about 12 feet before reaching the Belly Roll (above). Climb straight up, and belay in an alcove beneath an overhang. Climb out around the left side of the overhang and arrive midway along the Catwalk. This was first climbed by Hans Wittich, Walter Becker, and Rudolph Weidner, 27 June 1931.

Descent. It is very important to pay close attention to the direction of travel and notable features of the ascent as one proceeds, since the route, at least to the rappel, must be reversed to get back to the Upper Saddle. The value of this will be particularly evident in the case of bad weather. From the summit, downclimb about 300 feet to the SOUTHWEST to reach the top of the dihedral and chimney in the upper cliffband. After descending the chimney, continue another 100 feet to the southwest past the Catwalk to the top of the main rappel. Look for slings around a six-foot block about 40 feet to the south of the Catwalk. Rappel 120 feet to reach the scree ledge, then, scramble down to the Upper Saddle.

In the event of having a single, 50 meter rope, there is an alternate rappel route that begins on a ledge up to the southeast of the main rappel. From slings around a block, rappel 70 feet to a chockstone in a chimney. Make a second 70-foot rappel to reach the scree ledge just south of the main rappel finish. It also is reasonable in dry conditions to downclimb the entire Owen-Spalding route from the summit to the Upper Saddle.

The easiest line of descent from the Upper Saddle is to reverse the standard route and go back through the Eye of the Needle. Remember to head southwest at first to avoid the more difficult gully between the central rib and the Exum Ridge.

Exum Ridge

The Owen-Spalding and the Exum Ridge are the two most popular routes on the Grand Teton. Where the Owen-Spalding is the easiest line to the summit, being no more than a steep hike for most of its course, the Exum Ridge provides more of a climbing challenge. Solid rock, interesting route-finding, and commanding position along the south ridge of the highest peak in the range combine to yield one of the classic ascents of North American climbing. Most parties ascend only the upper, more moderate section of the ridge by traversing in along a ledge called Wall Street. The lower section is considerably steeper and more difficult but, if skill and experience allow, the entire 2500-foot ascent from the black dike is highly recommended.

The Exum or South Ridge is identified easily from the Lower Saddle as the serrated skyline ridge which descends from the summit and forms the right (east) margin of the broad gully above and north of the Lower Saddle. The upper section was first climbed by Glenn Exum who soloed the route as the maiden voyage of his climbing career on 15 July 1931. The entire ridge beginning from the black dike was first climbed by Jack Durrance and Ken Henderson on 1 September 1936.

The route is described in sequence beginning from the black dike. The ascent of the entire South Ridge is usually referred to as the Complete or Direct Exum Ridge. To descend from the summit it is possible to reverse the route to Wall Street but it is easier to downclimb the Owen-Spalding Route (q.v.).

11. Lower Exum Ridge
III 7

The Lower Exum Ridge is one of the great rock climbs on the Grand Teton. It features steep climbing on excellent rock, commanding position, and is fairly even in grade. The route is often climbed only to Wall Street.

Approach. From the Lower Saddle, follow the path northward through the tundra as for the Owen-Spalding route. At a point short of the black dike, break off to the right (east) and follow a faint path up over a promontory and contour along to a ledge 150 feet beneath the chockstone chimney of the first pitch. This chimney appears from the Lower Saddle as a large, west-facing dihedral. Most parties will want to rope up here.

The Route. An easy initial pitch works around to the left, up easy corners, and through a bulge (4) to reach the ledge beneath the chimney. A more difficult start takes a steep, left-facing dihedral which begins at a cairn on the next ledge up. The easiest way to reach the chimney is to continue farther along the black dike toward the Petzolt Ridge and follow a long, grassy ramp back left to the ledge.

1a. Climb the large chimney past two chockstones (6) to reach a pedestal at the top of another long ramp (135 feet).

1b. Climb the south-facing wall to the right of the chimney and work back left near the top (6). The cracks that continue straight up are more difficult (8 or 9).

2. Follow an easy ramp up to the left, then climb a dihedral and crack to a belay alcove just below a major step in the ridge (6, 150 feet). Move the belay up to the next steep section.

3. Jam up a handcrack to a wedged block, then work up and right to belay on a sandy ledge with a 10-foot detached flake (7, 100 feet).

4. Grunt up a V-shaped chimney with a wide crack (7) to a tunnel formed by a chockstone, climb out around either side (6), and go up a short crack to a small ledge at the base of the Black Face (65 feet).

5. Above rises a near-vertical face of exquisite black and gold rock that yields the hardest climbing on the route yet never lacks for good holds. Move up and right past a fixed pin, then follow a steep crack with more fixed pins to an alcove with a large, detached block (7, 110 feet).

6. Jam straight up a flared handcrack (7) to a fixed pin, traverse right, and ascend another crack to the top of Wall Street (7, 110 feet). It is possible (but not recommended) to avoid this pitch by working around to the left on easier terrain. At this point one may scramble off on Wall Street or continue to the summit via the Upper Exum Ridge.

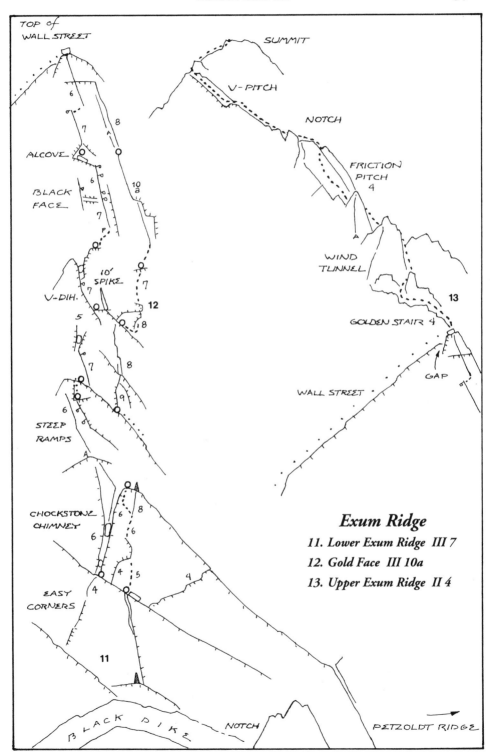

Exum Ridge

11. Lower Exum Ridge III 7

12. Gold Face III 10a

13. Upper Exum Ridge II 4

12. Gold Face
III 10a

This four pitch variation was first climbed by Teton rangers Renny Jackson and Jim Woodmency 27 June 1988. It features steep climbing on excellent Teton rock a short way right of the regular route. It may be reached via a short descent east from the top of the second pitch of the Lower Exum Ridge or by ascending the middle of three long ramps that angle up and left from the black dike. See topo.

13. Upper Exum Ridge
II 4

Here is the line of Glenn Exum's original solo of 1931. Follow the Owen-Spalding route to the gully just beyond the Eye of the Needle (q.v.), then scramble east to the crest of the central rib or, better, reach the crest at a gap a short way farther north. From here Wall Street is seen as a long, straight ledge that angles up and right to the skyline of the south ridge. Make a descending traverse into the scree gully to the east and scramble up a smaller side gully to get onto Wall Street. Walk up the broad, flat ledge to where it ends about 20 feet short of the ridge crest. Most parties will want to rope up here. Cross the gap (most easily via hand traverse) and belay on a big ledge with a commanding view. One is now on the south ridge of the Grand Teton about 1500 feet from the summit.

Beginning the friction pitch on the Upper Exum Ridge

Climb directly up the crest on solid, knobby rock (4) or work around to the northeast and ascend easy cracks back to the crest. This initial 60-foot step is called the Golden Stair. Scramble about 250 feet to a large tower that miraculously has escaped being named. Traverse right (east) for a ropelength, then go up either side of a steep gully/chimney system (sometimes icy) called the Wind Tunnel for two pitches. Now head up through terraces and a short chimney on the west side of the crest to reach a ledge at the base of a smooth, clean slab. One also may reach this point via a crack near the right edge of the crest.

The next ropelength is known as the Friction Pitch; it is the crux of the upper ridge and is rather poorly protected. Move up and slightly left on friction to two knobs, go up and right to a shallow groove, then upward to the top of the slab. Now scramble up and right to a small notch that may contain snow or ice. Work northwest along the right side of the crest for about 300 feet until it is possible to move left into a prominent, left-facing dihedral/ramp called the V-Pitch or Open Book. Pass the dihedral in 150 feet, then scramble across an easy section to the next step in the ridge. Move down a bit to the west and make an awkward lieback to pass this step.

Note that from the base of the step, it is possible to make a descending traverse northwest to the top of the Owen-Spalding rappel as a means of escape.

Continue up to another step that is passed via a short crack. Now follow the ridgecrest to the base of the summit block. Traverse east about 50 feet, then angle up over broken ground to the summit. There is a good alternate finish called the Horse. From the base of the summit block traverse around to its west side and climb up to a knife-edge ridge that is followed to the summit.

Petzoldt Ridge

The Petzoldt Ridge is the next large buttress to the right of the Exum Ridge. It is defined by the Beckey Couloir on the left and the Stettner Couloir on the right and, unlike the Exum Ridge, ends about halfway to the summit (roughly level with the top of Wall Street). The ridge features two classic routes on excellent rock either of which are fine alternatives to the more heavily traveled Exum route.

14. Direct Petzoldt Ridge
III 7

This is not a variation of the original Petzoldt Ridge route but an independent line that follows the crest of the buttress to its top. It was first climbed by Willi Unsoeld, LaRee Munns, James Shirley, Rodney Shirley, and Austin Flint on 30 August 1953.

Approach. Follow the black dike as for the Exum Ridge (above) but continue east to the bottom of the buttress.

The Route. Scramble directly up the ridge for about 200 feet to a good ledge or start up the Stettner Couloir and traverse left onto the same ledge.

1. Climb up through a slot with some fixed pins (7) and gain a ramp that is followed up and left. Negotiate a short chimney and belay up to the left.

2. Climb the face out and left around a black overhang (6) and belay at the top of a ramp/dihedral.

3. Follow a crack system to a belay beside a tunnel in the ridgecrest called the Window (6).

4a. Climb the crest of the ridge over the Window and continue up excellent rock to belay near a pinnacle (6).

4b. Go west through the Window and follow a ramp until a short, difficult crack can be climbed back to the ridgecrest (9).

5. Climb excellent rock to the right of the crest and belay on a ledge.

6. Climb directly up the crest and belay on a ledge.

7. Work up and right and gain the summit of the ridge.

Make a 50-foot rappel to the col on the north side of the ridge and choose from the following options:

The Ford Couloir. From the col, climb the snow couloir between the Exum Ridge and Buckingham Buttress. Continue on snow to the final section of the Exum Ridge and gain the summit. One may also traverse right after about 300 feet in the couloir and climb the upper Buckingham Buttress to the same fate. An ice axe and perhaps crampons will be needed for this finish.

The Petzoldt-Exum Traverse (6). From the col on the north side of the ridge, follow a ramp up to the west and join the Upper Exum Ridge route above the Golden Stair whence one may continue up the ridge to the summit or rappel 60 feet and descend via Wall Street.

15. Petzoldt Ridge
III 6

The Petzoldt Ridge route is one of the best moderate rock climbs on the Grand Teton and is an important alternative to the busy Exum Ridge. Through most of the summer, an ice axe will be needed either for the approach from the Lower Saddle or for ascending the Ford Couloir above the ridge. After mid summer, the Petzoldt-Exum Traverse may allow an ascent to the summit without snow travel.

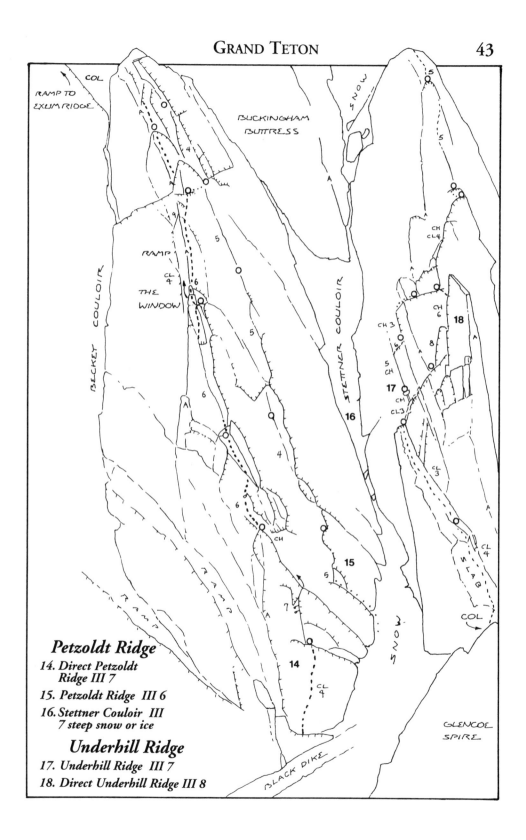

Petzoldt Ridge

14. *Direct Petzoldt Ridge III 7*

15. *Petzoldt Ridge III 6*

16. *Stettner Couloir III 7 steep snow or ice*

Underhill Ridge

17. *Underhill Ridge III 7*

18. *Direct Underhill Ridge III 8*

Approach. From the Lower Saddle, approach as for the Exum Ridge but continue east along the black dike into the Stettner Couloir along the east side of the buttress. Climb up the couloir (most likely on snow) until a ledge provides a traverse onto the face.

The Route. Note that there are many options on this route including the location of belays.

1. Traverse up onto the face, climb a black chimney (5), then work up slabs to belay beneath an open book.

2. Climb a large left-facing dihedral and belay beneath a roof (4).

3. Climb through the roof, go up a short left-facing corner, and follow a crack to a belay stance (5, 150 feet).

4. Follow the crack system to belay on a ledge left of a large roof (5, 150 feet).

5. Climb a gully or the ridge at left and belay beneath a short chimney (4, 120 feet).

6. Climb the chimney and scramble to the top of the ridge (3).

Rappel 50 feet into the col north of the ridge and choose from the options listed for the Direct Petzoldt Ridge (above).

16. Stettner Couloir
III 7, steep snow or ice

This is the steep couloir between the Petzoldt and Underhill Ridges. In early summer it provides an excellent snow and ice route to the summit. Mid to late season, some of the snow will be gone and rock climbing up to 7 in difficulty will be encountered. It was first climbed by Sam Younger and Albert Strube on 30 July 1933 apparently trying to find the Owen-Spalding Route. An ice axe and crampons are recommended along with a light rock climbing rack and a few ice screws.

Approach. Begin from the Lower Saddle as for the Exum Ridge (see above) but continue east along the dike past the bottom of the Petzoldt Ridge and head up into the couloir.

The Route. Follow the narrow couloir to where it branches beneath the Buckingham Buttress. The left fork leads over slabs to the col behind the Petzoldt Ridge; finish with the Ford Couloir (see above). The right branch goes straight up a steep, narrow ice couloir to the shallow col above the Underhill Ridge. Climb a short rock pitch (6) to get up onto the broad southeast face, then, climb snow or the Buckingham Buttress on the left and finish as for the Exum Ridge. A more direct finish can be made up either of two large chimneys at the top of the southeast face (4).

Underhill Ridge

The Underhill Ridge is the large buttress to the east of the Petzoldt Ridge. It is defined by the Stettner Couloir on the left but merges on the right with a large southeast-facing wall called the "east face" of the Grand Teton. There is a shallow col behind the top of the Underhill Ridge beyond which the southeast snowfields climb to the summit. The curiously shaped Otterbody Snowfield sits just north from the col and lends to identifying the ridge from the east. From the Lower Saddle, the Underhill Ridge is seen on the right skyline. An ice axe is recommended for ascents of this ridge at least until late summer.

17. Underhill Ridge
III 7

This route generally ascends the crest of the ridge but passes the difficult middle section on the west side. It was first climbed by Robert Underhill, Phil Smith, Paul Petzoldt, and William House on 15 July 1931.

Approach. Begin from the Lower Saddle as for the Exum Ridge (above) and follow the black dike to its high point at the Glencoe Col (the notch between Glencoe Spire and the Underhill Ridge).

The Route. From the col, scramble north across the bottom of a large slab to the base of a prominent tower. Follow cracks up the slab for 130 feet (cl4) and continue in a westerly direction to the top of a long ramp (cl3). Scramble up broken ledges on the west side of the ridge to the bottom of a short chimney.

1. Climb the chimney to a broad ledge (cl4). The difficult Underhill chimney begins from this ledge.

2. Do not climb the chimney but work around the corner to the left and climb an easier chimney until a bulge impedes upward progress. Make difficult moves right to a tiny ledge, then, crank up and right (7, no pro) into the first (Underhill) chimney and belay.

3. Climb the chimney for about 60 feet and belay on a ledge (4).

4. A long pitch up a chimney/dihedral leads to a ledge on the crest of the ridge (cl4).

5. Follow a crack up the middle of the narrow face and belay on a ledge near the top (5).

6. Climb a final short step (5) and follow easy rock to the top of the buttress.

Cross the col and climb snow or easy rock to a steeper section. A short pitch (6) brings one to the southeast snowfield which is followed to the summit block. Climb either of two moderate chimneys (4) or finish to the left as for the Exum Ridge.

18. Direct Underhill Ridge
III 8

This difficult variation stays more on the crest of the ridge and avoids the often wet chimneys of the regular route. From the Lower Saddle, a conspicuous tower of white rock can be seen on the skyline of the Underhill Ridge. Instead of traversing around onto the west side, the route climbs the chimney between the white tower and the main buttress, then, joins the original line. It was first climbed by William Buckingham, Steve Smale, Ann Blackenburg, Charles Browning, and Jack Hilberry on 30 August 1953.

The Route. Climb the initial slab and ramp of the regular route to where the ledge system goes around onto the west side. Do not go around to the west but scramble up and right on broken black rock to the bottom of the chimney that separates the white tower from the main ridge.

1. Climb the chimney which at first overhangs, then, becomes vertical (8). Continue past some chockstones to the notch between the tower and the main ridge and belay (6).

2. Climb up and left and join the regular route as shown in the topo.

East Ridge

19. East Ridge
III 7

The east ridge is the longest continuous feature of the Grand Teton. It begins from the south side of the terminal moraine of the Teton Glacier (about 10400) and climbs without significant interruption to the summit. The ascent of this ridge would be direct and relatively easy but for two large towers, the Molar Tooth and the Second Tower, both of which require a tricky and somewhat inobvious bypass. The ridge was attempted repeatedly before its first successful ascent by Robert Underhill and Kenneth Henderson on 22 July 1929. This was the first new line on the peak since the completion of the Owen-Spalding route in 1898. The East Ridge is a long and varied alpine route; an ice axe and crampons are recommended as well as a light rock climbing rack.

Approach. See Glacier Trail under Grand Teton (above). Hike up onto the terminal moraine of the Teton Glacier and proceed to its southern extreme. The route begins about 50 feet south from the crest of the moraine.

The Route. Scramble up the broad ridge keeping left of the crest for about 2000 feet to a large bowl beneath the Molar Tooth. The original route passed this formidable tower by an intricate traverse along its north side. The standard method now is to climb around its south side. From the bowl, two chimneys can be seen rising on the left. The route takes the left more broken chimney, however, the rock just to its left can be climbed for one pitch before the chimney is entered. Cut right at a ledge and continue in the upper chimney to a notch on the ridge called the Window. From here the Teepe Glacier can be seen below to the south. Descend a steep scree gully into the large couloir that rises from the glacier, then climb the couloir on snow or ice to the giant chockstone at its top. Pass the chockstone on the right and continue on snow or rock for another 75 feet to the notch above the Molar Tooth.

Climb a short, difficult pitch to get out of the notch (7), then work up and right and climb an easy chimney that leads to an alcove. Climb right out of the alcove and follow slabs for a couple of pitches, then angle up and left along ledges for several hundred feet and gain the crest of a spur that descends to the south from a pinnacle on the ridgecrest. Scramble around to the west side of this spur and climb a gully (snow-filled in early season) to the notch between the pinnacle and the summit of the Second Tower (on the west). The Second Tower now can be passed via ledges on its north side. About halfway across, downclimb about ten feet and pass behind a large flake, then climb a short chimney and continue on easier ground to the large platform at the west side of the Second Tower.

Climb steep scree or snow-covered slabs and gain the east snowfield. Climb directly to the summit block on snow or (in late season) climb rock to the right along the edge of the north face. At the top of the snowfield, climb directly up a steep, open chimney to the summit (6). Or climb way around to the left on snow and finish as for the Exum Ridge. Another option is to climb around to the right of the summit block and gain a chimney that leads to the north ridge just 100 feet beneath the summit.

North Side

20. North Face
IV 8

No collection of Teton classics would be complete without the North Face of the Grand Teton. Steeped in shadow on the cold side of the mountain, this complex mixed route is one of the great alpine challenges of the range. The face was first climbed on 25 August 1936 by Paul and Eldon Petzoldt; though they finished the route via the upper North Ridge, the ascent was made from Jenny Lake in a single day. The Direct North Face, which is now the standard line, ascends the very steep upper wall to the left of the North Ridge and was pieced together by different parties between 1941 and 1953. The entire route, including the first free ascent of the Pendulum Pitch and the final traverse into the V, was completed by Richard Emerson, Willi Unsoeld, and Leigh Ortenburger on 24 July 1953. The face is about 2500 feet high, tends to hold snow and ice on ledges, and has considerable hazard from rockfall on the initial pitches. Due to the great height of the face, speed of ascent is of the essence. An ice axe and crampons will be useful as well as full rock climbing gear up to three inches.

East Ridge of the Grand Teton, aerial view

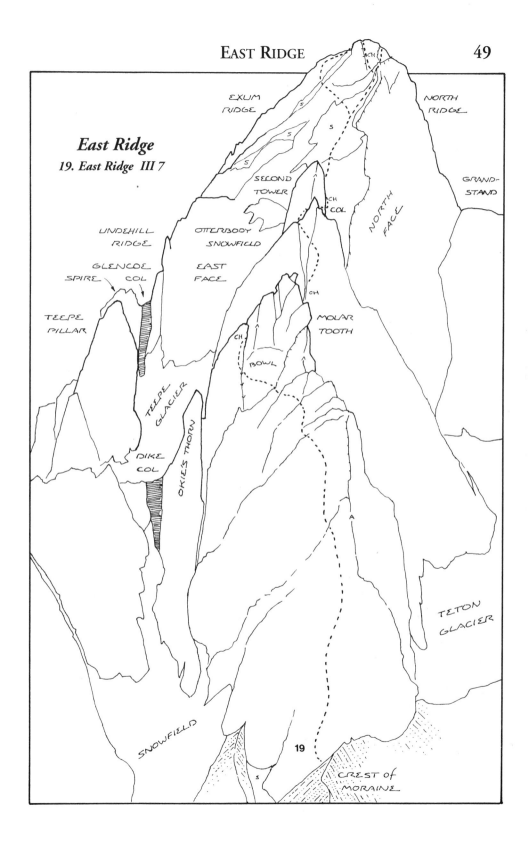

East Ridge

19. *East Ridge III 7*

EXUM RIDGE

NORTH RIDGE

S

S

S

S

SECOND TOWER

GRAND-STAND

CH COL

NORTH FACE

UNDEHILL RIDGE

OTTERBODY SNOWFIELD

EAST FACE

GLENCOE SPIRE COL

CH

TEEPE PILLAR

MOLAR TOOTH

CH

TEEPE GLACIER

BOWL

DIKE COL

OKIES THORN

A

TETON GLACIER

19

SNOWFIELD

S

CREST of MORAINE

North Face of the Grand Teton

Approach. Hike in via the Glacier Trail (see above) and climb to the top of the Teton Glacier. Take precaution for crevasses.

The Route. From the upper part of the Teton Glacier, note two deep chimneys left from the bottom of the Grandstand. Cross the moat and move up and left onto a ledge system at the base of the left chimney. The right (more westerly) chimney is loose and dangerous. It is possible to avoid most of the glacier and the moat crossing by ascending a long, diagonal ledge up to the base of the left chimney. Ascend the chimney for several moderate pitches, then move up and right along a ledge system to Guano Chimney (6), a deep cleft that leads to the First Ledge (see topo). Once up on the First Ledge, a bivouac can be made in a cave about 100 feet from the low end.

Scramble all the way to the west end of the First Ledge. Climb a steep, shallow chimney for about 130 feet (6) and belay. Then work up and left on easy friction to reach the Second Ledge. Scramble up to the right for three or four hundred feet until an obvious break leads directly up to the Third Ledge. Scramble another 400 feet or so up the Third Ledge to a right-facing dihedral just short of a bunch of rappel slings. This is the start to the Pendulum Pitch and is also a good place to exit the face in the event of nightfall or foul weather. To escape, rappel 120 feet to the Second Ledge, traverse up and westward to intersect the north ridge, then traverse the west face to the Upper Saddle.

Ascend the dihedral for about 75 feet (7), then work left on a sloping, tapering ledge, and make a blind traverse left (8). Climb up into a black alcove at the east end of the Fourth Ledge. Move the belay about 100 feet up the ledge to start the last difficult pitch. This is only about 50 feet from the north ridge. Traverse back left (east) to a small, right-facing dihedral and climb to its top. Now, traverse up and left on friction (7) for about 35 feet to reach the "V," a large recess in the upper north face from which a scramble of several hundred feet leads to the summit.

21. North Ridge
IV 7

If the ascent of any one route could qualify as the ultimate Teton experience, it may be the North Ridge of the Grand Teton. Likely the most difficult route in North America at the time of its first ascent, it has withstood the test of time and still is still considered a serious undertaking by experienced alpinists. The North Ridge was first climbed on 19 July 1931 by Robert Underhill and Fitiof Fryxell.

The route begins atop the Grandstand, the massive north shoulder of the Grand Teton that connects with Mount Owen via Gunsight Notch and forms the headwall of the Teton Glacier. Above the Grandstand, the route ascends a series of ramps and chimneys and finishes on the northwest arête. One also may finish with the last few pitches of the North Face route which adds notably to the overall difficulty of the ascent. The North Ridge is a long and complex alpine climb and typcially will require an ice axe, crampons, and mountain boots in addition to full rock climbing gear. Under rare late season conditions, the entire route from Valhalla Canyon will be dry and free of snow and may be done as a pure rock climb.

Approach. The Grandstand, from which the route proceeds, may be approached from the east via the Teton Glacier or from the west via Valhalla Canyon, the latter of which has become more popular.

A. To utilize the eastern option begin from Lupine Meadow, hike the Garnet Canyon Trail for several miles, and take the Glacier Trail to its end at Amphitheater Lake. From the lake, follow a climber's path north into Glacier Gulch, scramble up over the terminal moraine, slog up the Teton Glacier, and cross the moat to the Grandstand. The easiest line on the east face of the Grandstand is typically along its left margin and it is no piece of cake. One can expect rockfall from the north face and tricky route finding on steep snow and wet slabs. Just crossing the moat can be an ordeal.

B. To reach the top of the Grandstand from the west one has the same options as for the Black Ice Couloir. Perhaps the most practical venue is to make a very early start from the Lower Saddle and take the Valhalla Traverse (see above) around the west side of the Grand Teton to where it crosses the northwest ridge of the Enclosure. Follow a ramp down into Valhalla Canyon at the level of the second icefield of the Black Ice Couloir and make an ascending traverse onto the lower of three large ramps that diagonals up across the west face to the top of the Grandstand. Expect wet slabs, snow, ice, or all of the above along this ramp, however, much of this can be avoided in late season by staying as far left as possible. The ramp is a scramble in dry conditions.

The Route. From the top of the Grandstand, scramble up beside a large block and belay.

1. Go left behind the block, then work up and left (6) to a ledge that is followed into a gully. Scramble up the gully for about two pitches and belay on a bench (cl3).

2. Climb a short, steep wall of dark and shattered rock and continue to a shelf (usually snow-covered) at the base of the notorious Chockstone Chimney (4).

3. Climb directly up the steep chimney, pass the chockstone on the left (7 to 9 depending on who tells the story), and belay just above.

4. Continue up the chimney and belay at its top (6). This and the previous pitch may be done as one.

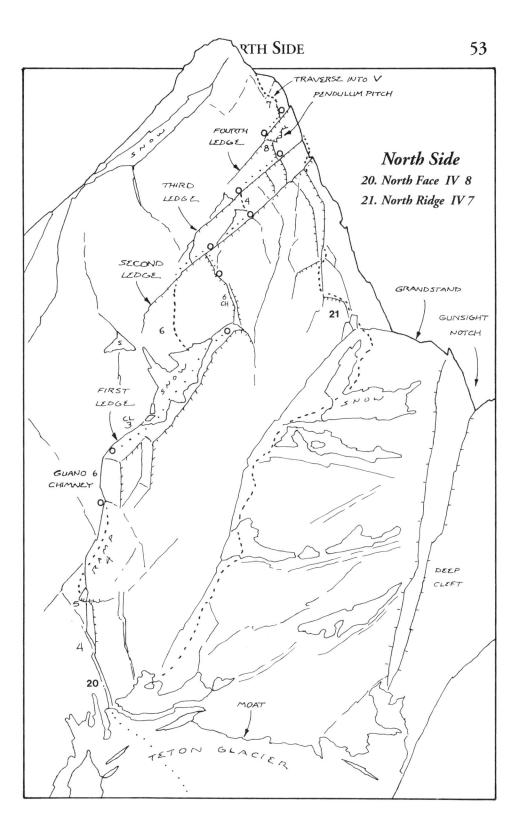

TRAVERSE INTO V

PENDULUM PITCH

7

FOURTH LEDGE

8

North Side

20. North Face IV 8

21. North Ridge IV 7

THIRD LEDGE

4

SNOW

SECOND LEDGE

6 CH

6

GRANDSTAND

21

GUNSIGHT NOTCH

S

SNOW

FIRST LEDGE

CL 3

GUANO 6 CHIMNEY

SNOW

RAMP

DEEP CLEFT

5

4

20

MOAT

TETON GLACIER

5. Climb a steep slab with poor protection, first going up and left to the arête (6 to 7), then back to the right to arrive at the Second Ledge of the North Face route (see topo). This pitch is very difficult if iced up and may require crampons.

6. Traverse up and right along the ledge to the west side of the ridge which at this point could be described as the northwest arête. Climb up to the Third Ledge of the North Face route and belay.

7. Follow a left-facing corner and chimney system to the Fourth Ledge of the North Face and belay (7).

8. Continue in the same system for another pitch (7) beyond which 400 feet of scrambling lead to the summit.

For a more rapid ascent from the Second Ledge (top of pitch five) it is possible to traverse right almost to the Great West Chimney and scramble to the summit. To escape the route from the Second Ledge, continue all the way across the west face to the Crawl of the Owen-Spalding and descend that route to the Lower Saddle.

22. Italian Cracks Variation
IV 7 or 8

This is an excellent alternative to the difficult and often icy chimney and slab pitches of the regular North Ridge route. The line follows a fairly direct series of cracks out on the north face, around to the left from the immense dihedral of the Chockstone Chimney. The name is derived from an ascent by George Montopoli (of apparent Italian descent) and Ralph Baldwin, however, A Complete Climber's Guide to the Teton Range credits the first ascent to Howard Friedman and Peter Woolen on 19 August 1971.

Begin about 15 feet from the east end of the long ledge above the first pitch and gully of the standard route.

1. Climb a wide crack for about 20 feet, then traverse 15 feet left into a long open chimney. Climb to the top of the chimney and belay on a ledge (7, 150 feet). It also is possible to climb straight up from the ledge (8) and merge left nearer to the roof.

2. Work up and around the left side of a roof and belay after 120 feet (7).

3. Moderate face climbing leads to the Second Ledge (5, 75 feet).

23. American Cracks
IV 9

This steep and difficult variation lies to the left of the Italian Cracks and poses another alternative to the standard North Ridge route. It was first climbed by Mike Colacino and Calvin Hebert on 7 July 1988.

From the top of the Grandstand, scramble up to a big block and belay.

1. Climb the first pitch of the standard route (6) but from the belay point in the gully system, drop down and left about ten feet and traverse 100 feet left along a ledge (cl4) to belay on a ramp.

2. Climb a short right-facing dihedral (8) followed by a wide handcrack (9) and belay at a good stance after 75 feet.

3. Continue up the handcrack and belay on a big ledge with a huge block (7, 90 feet). This is the same ledge from which the Italian Cracks begin.

4. From the big block, move down and left about 15 feet and climb a left-facing dihedral to the next ledge (7).

5. Move up and left and climb a long chimney that leans to the right. The crux is in passing some plate-like chockstones about halfway up the chimney (9). Belay on a ramp up and right from the end of the chimney.

6. Climb an easy crack up and right, then cut back left to the Second Ledge (4).

North Face Finish (IV 8). The direct finish to the North Face route adds three pitches of steep climbing to the standard route or to the Italian Cracks. This challenging combination was first completed from the standard North Ridge route by Jim Donini, Rick Black, and Michael Cole on 11 August 1976.

Looking east down the Second Ledge from the standard route, locate a black chimney between two right-facing dihedrals. Climb the black chimney (7) to the Third Ledge of the North Face route, then move the belay about 20 feet down to the east to the bottom of a right-facing dihedral. This is the Pendulum Pitch. Proceed as described above for the North Face.

Northwest Face

24. Black Ice Couloir
IV 7, steep ice and snow

The Black Ice Couloir is rightly thought of as *the* alpine ice climb in the Tetons. It was the first major route of its kind to be established in the range and now stands among the great classic climbs of North America. After at least two earlier attempts, it was fist climbed by Raymond Jacquot and Herb Swedlund on 29 July 1961.

The route is long and involved, hidden in the depths of the remote north-facing cleft between the west face of the Grand Teton and the north buttress of the Enclosure. There are three distinct icefields separated by sections of rock and a final, narrow chute that leads to the Upper Saddle. The couloir is difficult to reach by any

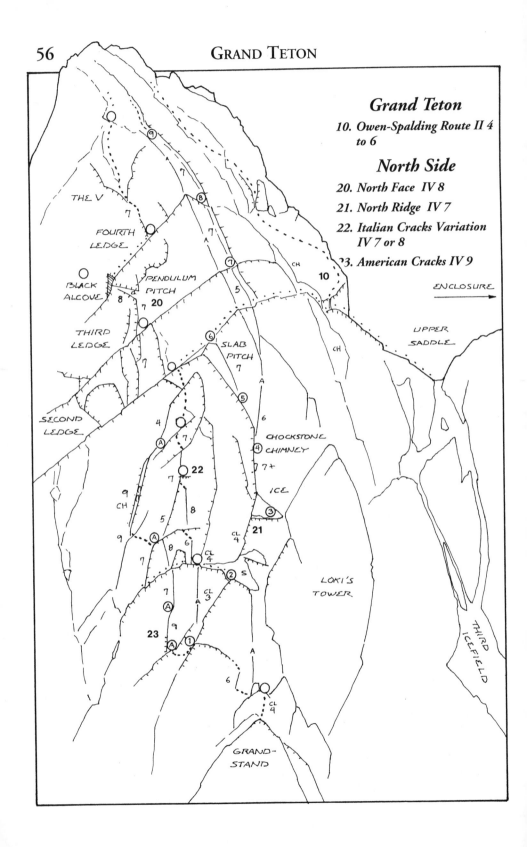

Grand Teton

10. Owen-Spalding Route II 4 to 6

North Side

20. North Face IV 8
21. North Ridge IV 7
22. Italian Cracks Variation IV 7 or 8
23. American Cracks IV 9

ENCLOSURE →

THE V

FOURTH LEDGE

BLACK ALCOVE

PENDULUM PITCH
20

THIRD LEDGE

UPPER SADDLE

SLAB PITCH

SECOND LEDGE

CHOCKSTONE CHIMNEY

ICE

22

21

LOKI'S TOWER

THIRD ICEFIELD

23

GRAND-STAND

approach and, once on the ice, escape is probably more of a risk than continuing to the top. There is some danger from rockfall, especially during warm weather and from climbers on the Owen-Spalding Route. The Black Ice Couloir requires mastery in route finding, the use of pitons and ice screws, and the ability to move quickly over mixed terrain with full alpine gear.

Approach. There are several logistical options for this ascent that depend upon path of approach and whether one plans a retrievable high camp, a carry-over, or a one-day marathon ascent. The most direct approach with the least hiking is via Valhalla Canyon (q.v.). The Black Ice Couloir begins from the head of this canyon and climbs for about 3000 feet to the Upper Saddle. If camp is made in the canyon, all overnight gear must be carried up the route. Thus, a one-day blitz might be preferable with this approach. Since the only reasonable descent is via the Owen-Spalding route, it is, however, possible to retrieve a camp in Valhalla Canyon by taking the Valhalla Traverse (see under Grand Teton) back to the north from the Lower Saddle.

The most popular two-day alternative is to hike the Garnet Canyon Trail and camp at the Lower Saddle. From there, the Valhalla Traverse is followed around into the Black Ice Couloir. Descent via the Owen-Spalding route brings one directly back to camp.

The Route from the Lower Saddle. Start early and follow the Valhalla Traverse around the west side of the Grand Teton to the northwest ridge of the Enclosure. Contour around to the north on a ledge that leads to a small basin or bowl. Cross the bowl (which likely will contain snow or ice) and follow a marginal ledge system around a buttress, back into the Enclosure Couloir. Cross the couloir and ascend the lower of two diagonal ramps that traverses the north buttress of the Enclosure and leads directly into the third icefield of the Black Ice Couloir. Note that three long ramps angle up and left across the lower west face of the Grand teton. The third icefield occupies the highest of these ramps which climbs for about 600 feet and opens into a basin near its top.

Above the third icefield, the couloir closes into a steep, narrow chute which provides the crux of the route. The ice reaches an angle of 70 degrees about 120 feet up into the chute, beyond which a partially protected belay niche will be found on the right. One last and easier pitch leads to the Upper Saddle. There are seven or eight pitches of ice from the bottom of the third icefield, some of which may be snow-covered in early season. Be alert for rockfall. The safest and most direct line is to follow the west margin of the ice and belay from pitons or ice screws along the north buttress of the Enclosure.

The Route from Valhalla Canyon. From the upper slopes of Valhalla Canyon it is possible to climb directly up into the Black Ice Couloir by ascending the first two icefields, angling right into the Enclosure Couloir, then proceding as described above. While this has the appeal of having done the whole thing, it also exposes the climber to the maximum hazard from rockfall. The wiser choice is probably to follow the line of the first ascent which, while bypassing the lower third of the main couloir, provides an excellent alpine ascent.

The Original Route. From upper Valhalla Canyon, work up and left and gain a ramp that leads directly into the second icefield of the Black Ice Couloir. To the right is the bottom of the Enclosure Couloir, ahead and to the left (east), three large ramps angle up and left onto the west face of the Grand Teton. Ascend the middle ramp (which sometimes begins with a narrow runnel of ice) for about 500 feet to an area of black rock. Now work up and right on broken rock and snow ledges for two pitches and arrive at the broad apron of the third icefield of the Black Ice Couloir. Climb up and across the icefield to the southwest and enter the narrow and final section of the climb (see above).

25. Visionquest Couloir
IV 7, steep ice

This steep and sensational ice climb ascends a narrow couloir that branches west from the Third Icefield of the Black Ice Couloir and tops out near the summit of the Enclosure. It first was climbed by Michael Stern and Stephen Quinlan, 10 August 1981.

The Grand Teton from Valhalla Canyon

The Route. Climb either version of the Black Ice Couloir to near the top of the Third Icefield. Head west up the initial chimney via mixed ice and rock (7) and continue up 60 degree ice in a narrow section of the couloir. After two pitches, the angle eases off slightly and the gully widens. Climb two more pitches of ice to a large chockstone that is passed on the right. Follow the upper couloir as it curves around to the top of the northwest ridge. The route from the Black Ice Couloir is about 600 feet long.

26. Enclosure Couloir
IV 7, moderately steep ice

The Enclosure Couloir slashes up and right across the north face of the Enclosure to the col between the Great Tower and the upper section of the northwest ridge. It is less steep and less subject to rockfall than the Black Ice Couloir and is one of the most popular alpine ice climbs in the range. It was first climbed by Peter Lev, William Read, and James Greig on 22 July 1962. Bring typical gear for snow and ice climbing plus a light rack up to a #3 Friend.

Approach. It is possible to begin the climb from the second icefield of the Black Ice Couloir but this necessitates an approach via Valhalla Canyon or a descent to the icefield from the Valhalla Traverse. The more pleasant and logical option is to follow the Valhalla Traverse (see under Grand Teton) to its end at the Enclosure Couloir about 200 feet above the second icefield (also see Black Ice Couloir above).

The Route. Climb 50 degree snow or ice (depending on season) for about 800 feet to the sharp col between the Great Tower of the northwest ridge and the steep upper rib. Continue with the Northwest Ridge route (see below) or rappel and downclimb the west face of the Enclosure to the Valhalla Traverse. To do the rappels, descend a ledge system a good way to the south and make two long rappels from slings. Continue to downclimb over steep, loose terrain to the Valhalla ledge system.

27. Northwest Ridge
III 7

The Northwest Ridge, climbed in its entirety from Cascade Canyon, is the longest route on the Grand Teton. However, only the section above the Valhalla Traverse is described here because it is an excellent rock climb and because its upper half is the logical conclusion to the Enclosure Couloir. Note that this ridge does not lead to the summit of the Grand Teton but to the summit of the Enclosure. The entire ridge was first climbed by Jack Durrance and Michael Davis, 8-10 August 1938.

Approach. Hike the Garnet Canyon Trail to the Lower Saddle, then, follow the Valhalla Traverse around to the base of the northwest ridge (see under Grand Teton).

The Route. Identify a left-facing dihedral with a good crack (see topo).

Aerial view of Grand Teton from the northwest. The Enclosure is at right.

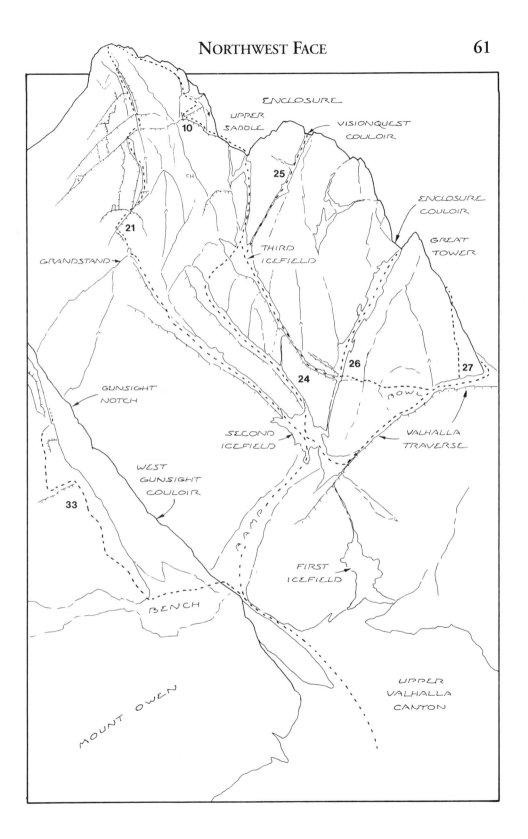

ENCLOSURE

UPPER
SADDLE

VISIONQUEST
COULOIR

10

25

ENCLOSURE
COULOIR

GREAT
TOWER

21

THIRD
ICEFIELD

GRANDSTAND

GUNSIGHT
NOTCH

26

27

24

BOWL

SECOND
ICEFIELD

VALHALLA
TRAVERSE

WEST
GUNSIGHT
COULOIR

33

RAMP

FIRST
ICEFIELD

BENCH

MOUNT OWEN

UPPER
VALHALLA
CANYON

Photo: Jeff Splitigerber

Richard Rossiter in the crux of Black Ice Couloir

1. Climb the dihedral which is difficult for the first 25 feet, then continue up easier corners to a belay in black rock. An intermediate belay can be made on this long pitch.

2. Climb through a slot and belay on a good ledge (4).

3.- 5. Traverse right and up over excellent rock to the col at the top of The Enclosure Couloir. Cross the col to the south and belay beneath the next steep step in the ridge.

6. Climb a steep crack (left of the arete of the buttress) that angles up and left to a belay beneath a roof (7).

7. Work around the right end of the roof (6), climb to the top of the wall, and continue up to belay behind the inital buttress.

8. Climb a crack on the right past a roof, then, scramble over black rock and belay at left.

9. Scramble up to a steep yellow wall and finish with a move of aid at a fixed pin. The final wall can be avoided via a talus gully of black rock to the left.

Scramble 150 feet northeast to reach the summit of the Enclosure.

Descent. From the summit of the Enclosure, scramble down to the Upper Saddle and descend the Owen-Spalding Route to the Lower Saddle.

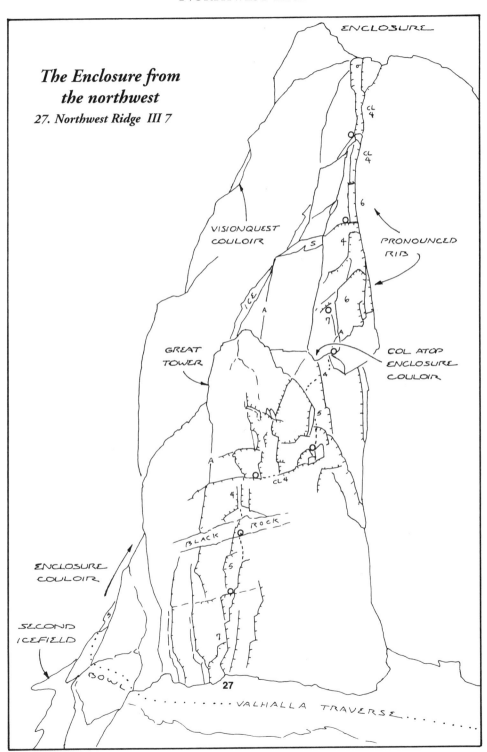

The Enclosure from the northwest

27. Northwest Ridge III 7

ENCLOSURE

CL 4

CL 4

6

VISIONQUEST COULOIR

5

4

PRONOUNCED RIB

ICE

A

6

7

A

GREAT TOWER

COL ATOP ENCLOSURE COULOIR

4

5

A

CL 4

4

BLACK ROCK

5

ENCLOSURE COULOIR

SECOND ICEFIELD

3

7

BOWL

27

VALHALLA TRAVERSE

Garnet Canyon, Disappointment Peak Buttresses below the Cathedral Group
of the Grand, Owen, and Teewinot

Disappointment Peak

As far as Teton summits are concerned, we could say that Disappointment Peak lives up to its name. With the loftiest peaks of the range towering above to the west, this stumpy wedge of rock attracts little attention from mountaineers and tourists. This is not to say that the view from the summit is dreary; it is decidedly spectacular, and the ascent from Amphitheater Lake is a splendid alpine scramble–the same scramble, in fact, made by Phil Smith and Walter Harvey who inadvertently bagged the first ascent of Disappointment Peak on a thwarted attempt to climb the Grand Teton, 20 August 1925. In another, flatter place, the peak itself might be a national park, but literally hidden against the backdrop of the mighty central Tetons, it goes almost completely unnoticed...except by rock climbers.

Disappointment Peak is situated immediately southeast of the Grand Teton and forms the divide between Glacier Gulch and Garnet Canyon. It has a very steep, 1000-foot northeast face that has seen some climbing activity, but the main attraction is the long row of south-facing arêtes and buttresses directly above the Garnet Canyon Trail. Due to this proximity, a warm southern exposure, and high visibility to climbers approaching the Grand Teton, many routes have been done on these features. Where some have fallen into obscurity, a few routes have withstood the test of time and now are considered classics. Of them all, a solitary line stands out and has gained a wide reputation as one of the best rock climbs in the Tetons. Long before most climbers make their first journey to these mountains, they are aware of a route called Irene's Arête.

28. Irene's Arête
III 8 or 10a

As one hikes westward from the Platforms in Garnet Canyon, an unusually sharp, clean fin of rock draws the eye from the other less well-formed features on the northern skyline. This is Irene's Arête which was first climbed by John Dietschy and Irene Ortenburger on 10 July 1957. Though the route is not terribly difficult, the climbing is fairly sustained, the rock is beautiful, and unlike many other Teton outings, there are no dud pitches. Rack up to 3 inches. The more difficult "direct" variations are credited to Jim Olson and Mark Chapman from an ascent on 2 July 1970.

Approach. Hike the Garnet Canyon Trail all the way to the last of some 18 switchbacks below Petzoldt Caves. Continue west past a cliffband on the right, then about 150 feet before reaching the top of Spalding Falls, turn right on a faint footpath that climbs steeply up talus to the north. Work back around to the top of the cliffband where a broad, wooded ledge leads about 200 yards east to the base of Irene's Arête. The initial grove of trees is a good place to leave extra gear. Just east of the grove, follow the ledge down around the foot of a small buttress and up the far side to a notch with a large pine tree; this point is directly beneath Irene's Arête. Turn north, then work up and left along ramps and short cliffs to a ledge that is just west of the continuous aspect of the arête (cl4).

The Route. Belay on the ledge or pull around onto the east side of the arête and belay atop a pedestal.

1. Climb discontinuous cracks up and right from the pedestal (7) and belay in a tiny alcove (100 feet).

2. Jam straight up a steep handcrack with fixed pins (8), and belay on a big ledge (100 feet). Move the belay north to the base of the arête.

3a. Climb about 10 feet just left of the crest, then pull around to the right into a marginal crack system (7). Work straight up via a dihedral in black rock, pull around to the left side of the crest, and jam another 30 feet up to a good ledge on the right side of the crest (7, 165 feet).

3b. Begin down to the right from the arête in an area of white, decomposed rock. Jam a crack up through a roof (9) and merge left with the regular line.

Caves Arête (left) and Irene's Arête viewed from
the Garnet Canyon Trail.

4a. Make strenuous moves up and left past a fixed pin (8), then climb beautiful, steep rock along the arête to a black roof (6). Pull right into the middle of the roof, crank up on big jugs, and exit the roof at a two-inch white crystal (8). Continue up into a groove (7) and work slightly left to belay on a good ledge at the base of a 90 degree dihedral (160 feet).

4b. Begin just right of the belay and jam a finger crack up to the black roof (8).

4c. At the roof it is possible to stay left and climb the arête (7, no pro) to the belay.

Photo: Joyce Rossiter

Irene's Arête, pitch four

5a. Jam and stem up the dihedral (9), hand traverse up and right, then power up a groove (7) to a lower angle section of the arête. Run the rope all the way to the notch at the next vertical step and belay (165 feet).

5b. Work around to the left of the dihedral and up to the arête (7).

5c. From the belay, pull right around the arête and climb a good crack up to the low-angle section (8).

6a. Though there are easier alternatives, the direct finish is well protected and is the line of choice. From the highest point, stem across the gap to the vertical wall and undercling/lieback up into a dihedral that is followed to the end of roped climbing (10a, 70 feet). A #3.5 Friend or equivalent may be used here.

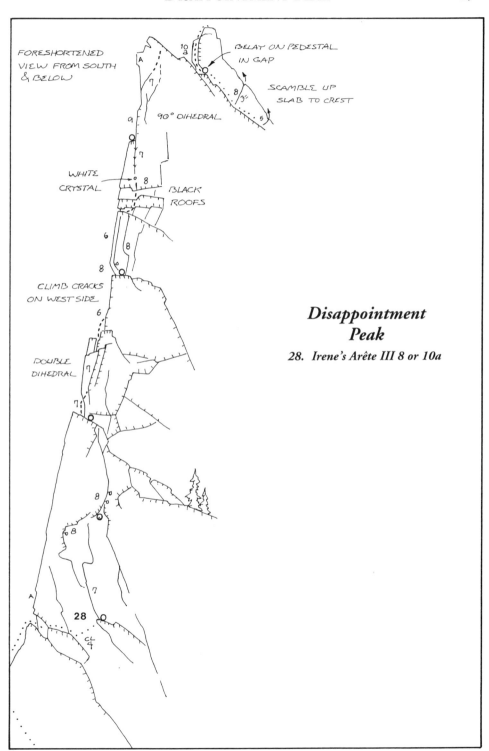

FORESHORTENED
VIEW FROM SOUTH
& BELOW

10 a

A

7

BELAY ON PEDESTAL
IN GAP

8
3"

SCAMBLE UP
SLAB TO CREST

5

9

90° DIHEDRAL

7

WHITE
CRYSTAL

8

BLACK
ROOFS

6

8

8

CLIMB CRACKS
ON WEST SIDE

6

DOUBLE
DIHEDRAL

7

7

8

8

7

A

28

CL
4

Disappointment Peak

28. *Irene's Arête III 8 or 10a*

6b. Move down the gully about 60 feet to the east and climb a steep fist crack to scrambling terrain (8).

6c. Descend the gully about 150 feet to the east and make a few steep moves (5) to reach a low-angle slab. From here, scramble northwest to the ridgecrest.

Descent A. Scramble along the crest of the ridge, first on the right, then on the left to avoid a tower. Once on the slopes of Disappointment Peak, follow a faint path westward through scrub evergreens to the SECOND gully west of Irene's Arête. This is the Southwest Couloir (cl4) and it is the easiest way to return to the base of the climb and the Caves area. About a third of the way down the gully, the descent is blocked by a large chockstone. Rappel 60 feet from slings or pass it by scrambling across to the east and downclimbing an easy chimney. Continue down the steep, loose gully staying mostly to the right but avoid a right-hand branch that leads more to the west.

Descent B. Work down to the east to a plateau that is above and west-southwest of Amphitheater Lake. Stay to the south of the Spoon Couloir (the long, narrow gully) and descend to the east via ledges and short cliffs until it is possible to curve around north to the lake. Find the Glacier Trail at the east end of the lake and follow it to its junction with the Garnet Canyon Trail. See Lake Ledges below. The Grand Teton Quadrangle (map) will be useful when making this descent for the first time.

29. Open Book
III 9

A thousand feet or more to the right (east) of Irene's Arête, the South Central Buttress forms a large summit that rises above the skyline of the ridge. The next feature to the right of this is called Grunt Arête, perhaps for the route of the same name or perhaps the other way around. About 100 feet right of the arête, a large open book dihedral splits the face and poses a fine rock climb. The long crack system in the corner of the dihedral was first climbed by Philip Jacobus and Steve Larsen on 21 August 1963. The first all free ascent was made by Jim Donini and Mike Munger on 26 June 1977.

Approach. Hike the Garnet Canyon Trail to the point where it effectively ends at the stream in the narrows of the canyon. Just across the stream is the area known as the Platforms, now closed to camping. To the west is a jumble of giant boulders among which the trail is obscured. Plainly visible to the north of this point is Grunt Arête and the Open Book. Hike up talus and easy ledges to the west of the arête, then traverse right onto a big ledge at the bottom of the dihedral.

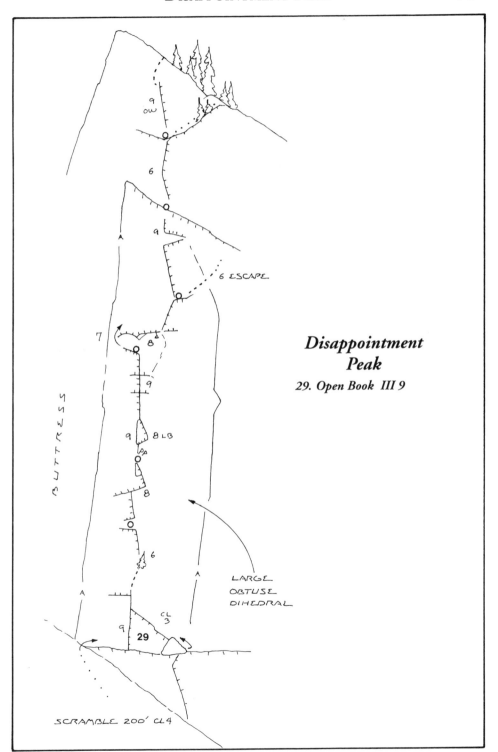

*Disappointment
Peak*

29. Open Book III 9

The Route. Belay at a big flake to the right of the corner.

1. Climb up and left along a ramp (cl3) or take a more difficult direct start to the left (9). Then, climb straight up past a small tree and belay beneath a roof (6).

2. Climb up and pass a roof on the right (8) via undercling and lieback, then belay above a detached flake from two pins.

3. Climb up around either side of a flake (easier on the right), then continue up the thin crack past two small roofs (9) and belay on a ledge beneath a large overhang.

4. Traverse about 20 feet right beneath the roof until it is possible to escape upward at an exposed slot (8). Supposedly, it is possible to pass this roof on the left (7) but details are not available. Climb a short left-facing dihedral and belay. It is possible to escape the route by climbing up and right from this belay (5 or 6).

5. Continue up the left-facing dihedral and turn a roof on the left (9). Belay above on a good ledge.

6. Continue up the same corner system (6) to another ledge from which one can scramble off to the right.

7. Climb a rotten left-facing dihedral with a wide crack to the top of the face (9).

Descent. From the top of the climb, traverse north, then drop down to the east. Downclimb a chimney past some chockstones and descend a large gully south into Garnet Canyon. It is perhaps easier to scramble down to Surprise Lake and follow its outlet south into Garnet Canyon. Another alternative from Surprise Lake is to hike out via the Glacier Trail.

30. Lake Ledges
II Class 4

This is the route taken on the first ascent of Disappointment Peak as described above. From Amphitheater Lake, hike straight west and scramble up through cliffs and ledges following the line of least resistance for about 500 feet. The usual line of ascent lies a short way left of the Spoon Couloir, the narrow gully that spans the cliff. When filled with snow, this gully is a good moderate snow climb. From the top of the cliffs, hike northwest up the long talus slope and scramble up easy rock to the summit.

Irene's Arête, pitch three

Mount Owen and the Teton Glacier,
aerial view from the southeast

Mount Owen

FROM THE SOUTHEAST SHORE OF JENNY LAKE, Mount Owen (elevation 12928) is completely eclipsed by Teewinot. But viewed from the plains to the northeast it towers above Cascade Canyon in a dramatic cluster of peaks known as the Cathedral Group. Mount Owen, the second highest of the Teton summits, forms the north wall of the Teton Glacier Cirque. It is connected at the southwest to the Grand Teton via Gunsight Notch and the Grandstand, and connected on the east, via a long ridge, to Teewinot Mountain. This graceful diadem of jagged ridges and terraced snowfields was the last of the great Teton peaks to be climbed, and its first ascent by the east ridge created one of the finest alpine routes in the range.

31. The East Ridge
II 6

This aesthetic and satisfying route ascends a deep couloir to a col on the east ridge, then continues up terraced snowfields and the prominent upper buttress to the summit. The ascent develops tremendous relief and scenic grandeur as one moves up the final pitches toward the summit knob. Across a void to the south, the north face of the Grand Teton looms larger than life, while to the north, Cascade Creek and the southwest ridge of Storm Point appear in miniature 5500 feet below. The route was first climbed by Kenneth Henderson, Robert Underhill, Phil Smith, and Fritiof Fryxell on 16 July 1930. Bring an ice axe and a modest rock climbing rack up to a #3 Friend. Check with the rangers on the advisability of crampons.

Approach. Hike the Glacier Trail to Surprise Lake which is the traditional campsite for the ascent. Continue to Amphitheater Lake and pick up a climber's path that leads north to a notch in the east ridge of Disappointment Peak where Mount Owen comes into full view. The east ridge forms the right skyline. The prominent gendarme down to the east of the upper snowfield is the East Prong. Traverse west along a ledge with a steel cable for a handrail into Glacier Gulch. Contour around to the north and climb the moraine up onto the Teton Glacier.

The Route. Cross the lower Teton Glacier and enter the initial section of the Koven Couloir (the gully that leads to the col west of the East Prong. Kick steps in snow (scree in late season) up to a small waterfall. Pass this feature on the left and attain a broad, typically snow-covered bench. Above the bench, climb the steeper upper couloir to the col west of the East Prong. This may be done directly up steep snow or via fourth class terrain on the left side of the couloir. Now head straight west and encounter the next obstacle, a 120-foot rockband. Of several options, the easiest is to traverse about 50 feet north from the crest of the ridge and climb a deep chimney to the upper snowfield. The chockstone near the top of the chimney may be passed on either side.

From here the climb becomes more dramatic. Ascend the eastern crest of the snowfield to the base of the upper east ridge where several options exist for passing the steep initial buttress.

A. Perhaps the easiest is to continue on snow for several hundred feet along the north side of the ridge until it is possible to work up and left along ramps and ledges to gain the crest of the ridge.

B. A more difficult and aesthetic option is to climb directly up the east arête of the buttress via a 60-foot left-facing dihedral (7) that leads to a belay at a fixed pin. From the pin traverse right about 20 feet and scramble a full rope-length up a shallow gully (cl4) that leads to the ridge crest.

C. A third option is to climb a moderate chimney system on the south side of the ridge (see topo).

Once on the crest of the ridge proceed westward up easy slabs for a couple of hundred feet to a ledge with slings. Then, climb a moderate gully on the south side of the crest for a full rope-length to an alcove at the base of the summit knob. The final event is a steep, 60-foot slab. Begin this last pitch to the right, work up and left to a small flake (6), traverse left on a down-sloping ledge, then shoot straight for the top. The last 30 feet are easier. Three, three-eighths-inch stoppers can be used at strategic points.

Descent. It is relatively easy to rappel down the East Ridge and the Koven Couloir as a series of sling anchors exist for this purpose. Two ropes are required. It also is possible to downclimb the Koven route beginning from the west side of the summit knob (see next page).

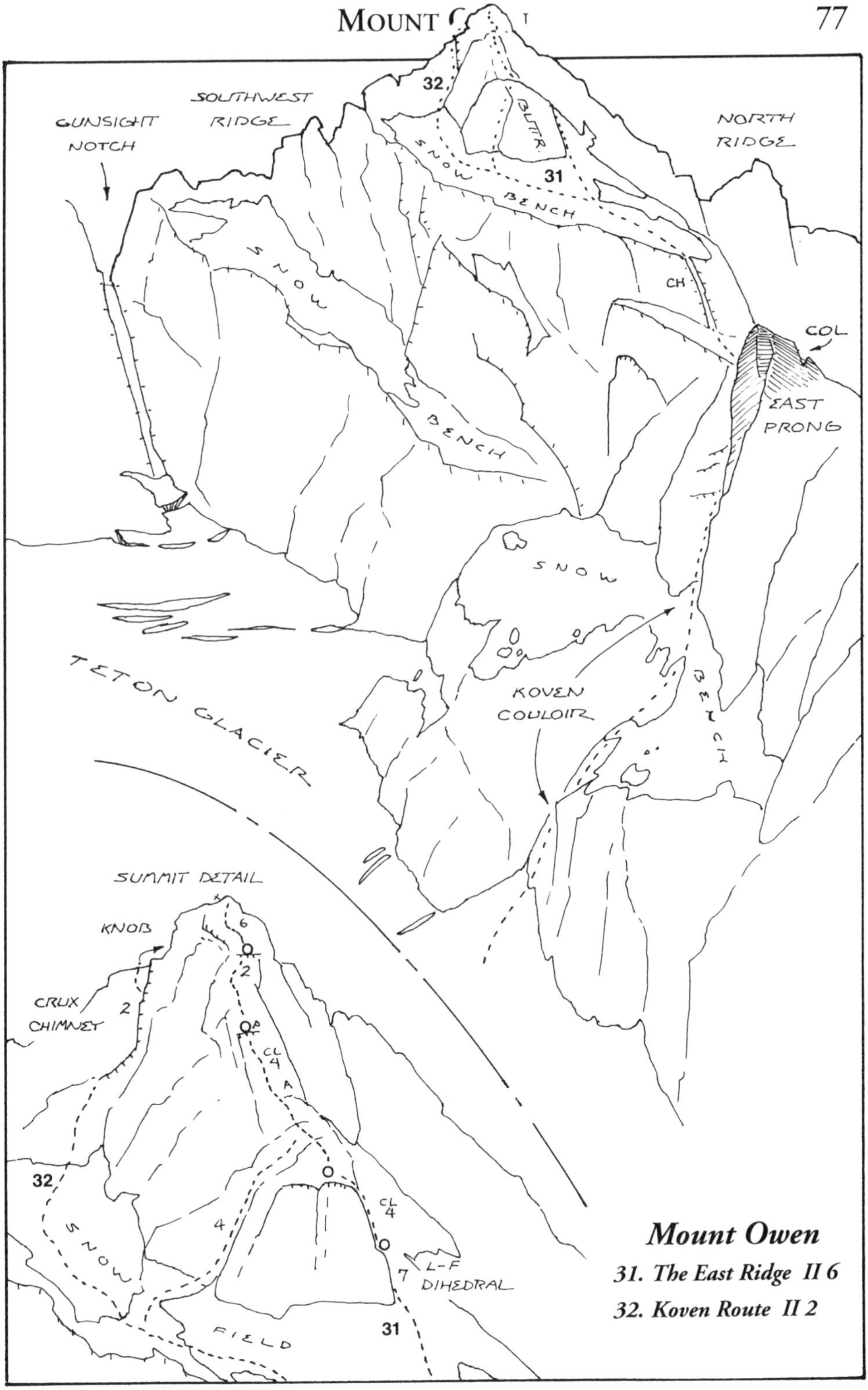

GUNSIGHT NOTCH

SOUTHWEST RIDGE

NORTH RIDGE

32

COULTR

31

SNOW BENCH

CH

COL

S N O W

EAST PRONG

B E N C H

SNOW

BENCH

KOVEN COULOIR

TETON GLACIER

SUMMIT DETAIL

KNOB

6

2

CRUX CHIMNEY

2

CL 4

A

32

O

CL 4

SNOW

4

O

7

L-F DIHEDRAL

FIELD

31

Mount Owen

31. The East Ridge II 6
32. Koven Route II 2

32. Koven Route
II 2

On 20 July 1931, Theodore and Gustav Koven, Paul Petzoldt, and Glen Exum reached the summit by a variation of the original East Ridge and discovered the easiest route up Mount Owen. In early to mid summer this is a sweeping snow climb with a short stretch of rock at the top; in late season, more rock and scree will have to be traveled.

The Route. Begin with the East Ridge route and follow it all the way to the upper snowfield. Instead of climbing up to the base of the rock buttress, traverse left along the bench all the way to slabs and ledges near the southwest ridge. Head northwest up a gully to a steep corner. Ascend a 40-foot chimney in the right wall (crux), then move left up steep slabs to reach the crest of the southwest ridge. Follow an easy ledge system north to an area of black rock. Now work up and right to the base of the deep, west chimney which is followed for about 40 feet to the summit.

33. Serendipity Arête
IV 7

This provocative route ascends the steep western arête of Mount Owen which, viewed from the Black Ice Couloir, forms the left skyline of the peak. The pinnacled arête may be identified by a large left-facing dihedral on its lower buttress and by its termination at the highest tower along the north ridge. The first ascent was completed on 8 August 1959 by William Buckingham, Rick Medrick, Sterling Neale, and Frank Magary; first free ascent 14 July 1965 by Henry Mitchell and George Griffin. Rack up to a #4 Friend.

Approach. The most reasonable approach to the west side of Mount Owen is via Cascade Canyon and Valhalla Canyon (see under Grand Teton). Hike into the upper reaches of Valhalla Canyon until directly beneath Gunsight Notch, the sharp break in the ridge between Mount Owen and the Grand Teton. Turn east and continue up snow or scree toward the notch until it is possible to traverse left (north) across a smaller gully onto a large bench above a cliffband. It also is feasible to scramble up the smaller gully. Continue north along the bench to the bottom of the main buttress (just past a stonefall gully).

The Route. Scramble up slabs for several hundred feet to the base of the first steep tower. Traverse left across broken ledges for half a rope to start the first hard pitch. Note that intermediate belays can be made on some of the longer pitches.

1. Climb straight up past the left end of a roof (4), hand traverse up and right along the top of a slab, and continue right around the crest to the base of an open chimney (5).

2. Climb the chimney for about 30 feet, then step left and jam a clean crack until it is possible to move back into the chimney (7) and continue to a good ledge. It may be possible to climb a crack to the right of the chimney.

3. Climb straight up a slab, jam a hand crack through a roof (7), and belay above on a ledge.

Scramble to the top of the first tower (cl4).

4. Traverse a spectacular knife-edge ridge to the base of the smaller second tower and belay on a ledge (4).

5. Traverse 35 feet down and right along a narrow ledge and belay beneath a crack and chimney system in black rock.

6. Jam and stem up the cracks and belay in the notch behind the second tower (7).

7. Climb an easy crack above the belay to gain the top of the third tower.

Scramble several hundred feet up the left side of the crest and gain a big ledge halfway up the fourth and final tower.

8. Climb up loose flakes and blocks on the left (north) side of the arête and belay at a stance after 150 feet (7).

9. Move right to the crest. Climb straight up, then scramble up easy rock on the right side of the crest to the top of the fourth tower (4). This is the highest tower on the north ridge of Mount Owen.

Scramble down to the col between the fourth tower and summit block.

10. Climb a steep chimney which may require a move of aid (7, A0).

Follow the north ridge for several hundred feet to the summit or traverse out onto the west face and climb the big west chimney of the Koven Route (cl4).

From the summit, one may descend to the east via the East Ridge or the Koven Route (see above). However, if a camp was left in Valhalla Canyon, which is likely, the West Ledges (II 2) must be downclimbed: Descend the west chimney of the Koven Route to the ledge that crosses the west face, then downclimb the southwest ridge toward Gunsight Notch and reverse the route indicated in the topo. With good navigating, the entire descent can be made without rappels. Do not start down the west side of the southwest ridge too soon; rappel slings to facilitate this blunder will found along the crest. Ignore these and continue to the U-notch as indicated.

Mount Owen as seen from the Black Ice Couloir.
Serendipity Arête is at left.

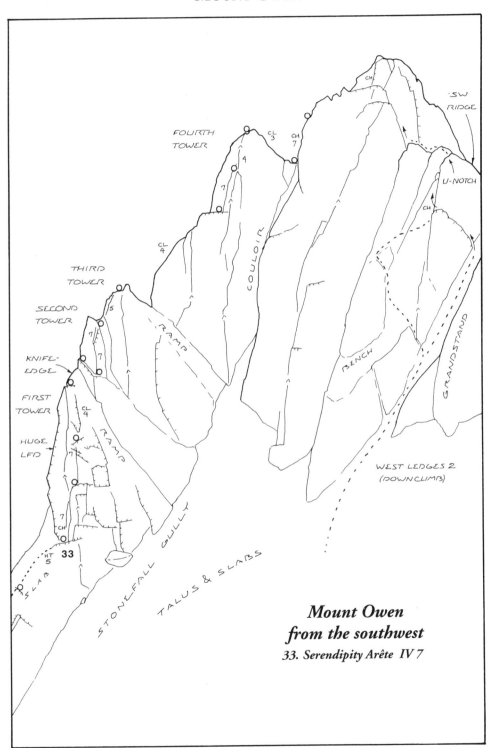

*Mount Owen
from the southwest*
33. Serendipity Arête IV 7

Teewinot Mountain above Jenny Lake

Teewinot Mountain

ONE OF THE MOST BEAUTIFUL AND COMPELLING PEAKS in the Teton Range is Teewinot., 12325 It is the only alpine peak wholly visible from the main visitor area at Jenny Lake and, with its serrated skyline ridge and shining snow couloirs, it completely dominates the landscape. Its prominent position along the eastern slope of the range, directly above the Lupine Meadow parking area, also makes Teewinot the most accessible of the major Teton summits.

34. East Face
II Class 4, moderate snow

A triangular, timbered ridge called the Apex climbs Class 4 toward the middle of the east face of Teewinot; above, a broad couloir slashes up and right to a notch at the south side of the summit. These features define the East Face route, one of the most direct and enjoyable alpine outings in the Tetons. What it lacks in technical challenge is more than offset by the brevity of approach, direct line to the summit, and peerless view of the Grand Teton and Mount Owen. In early season the route is a long snow climb requiring an ice axe and mountain boots, but by mid august the 5600-foot ascent may go entirely on rock. A rope and light rack are recommended for this climb as some parties may want to belay the steeper sections. The first documented ascent was made by Fritiof Fryxell and Phil Smith, 14 August 1929.

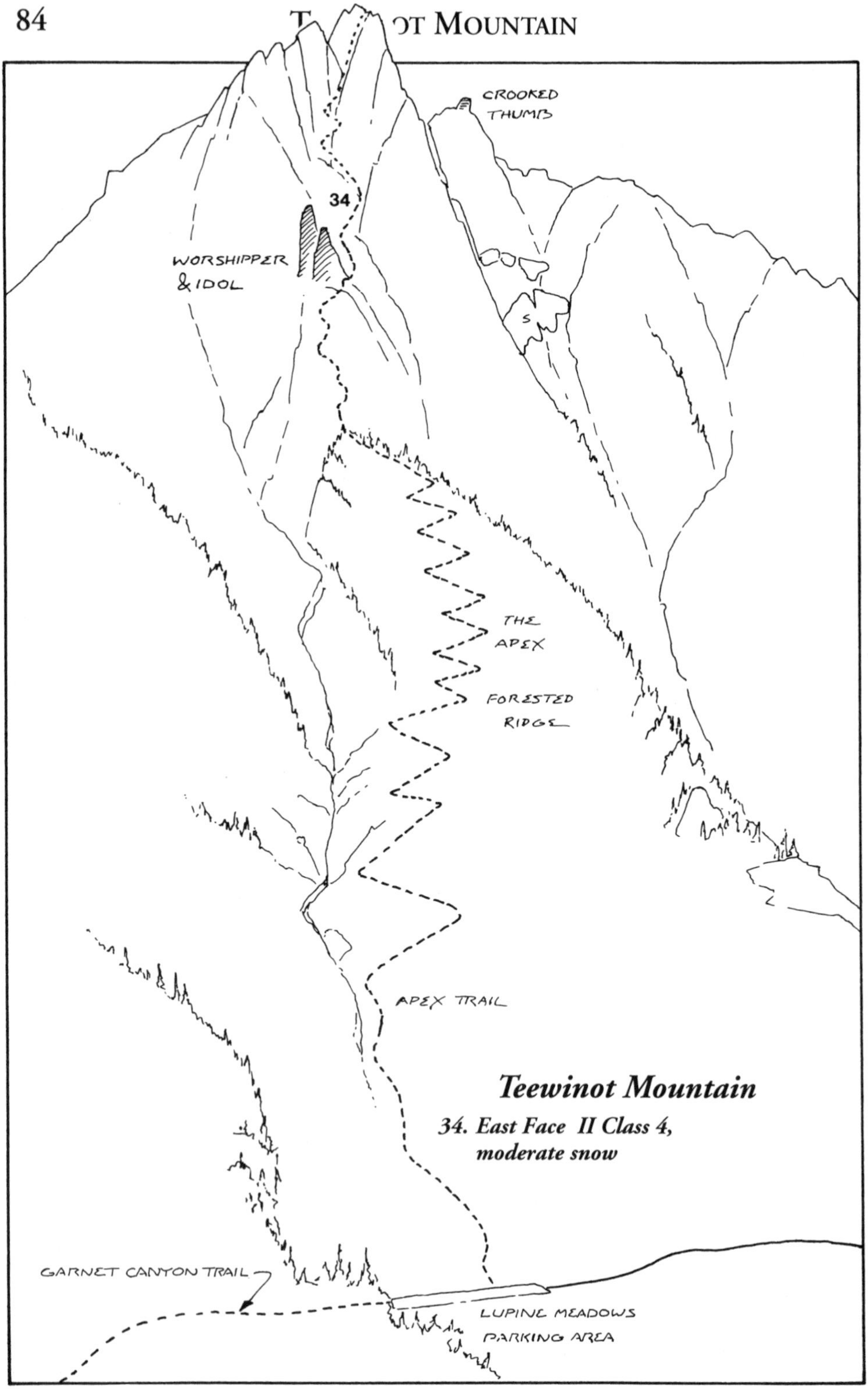

CROOKED
THUMB

34

WORSHIPPER
& IDOL

S

THE
APEX

FORESTED
RIDGE

APEX TRAIL

Teewinot Mountain

34. East Face II Class 4,
moderate snow

GARNET CANYON TRAIL

LUPINE MEADOWS
PARKING AREA

The Route. The Apex Trail begins along the west side of the Lupine Meadow parking area about 150 feet from its north end. Follow this trail westward, first through a tangle of scrub vegetation, then up the forested ridge. After an interminable number of switchbacks, one reaches the top of the Apex. The trail continues westward along a wooded ridge, then climbs steeply to a talus field just beneath two prominent gendarmes known as the Worshipper and the Idol (higher). Angle up and right into the broad couloir where one is likely to begin on snow. In late season, a vaguely discernible path may be followed up ramps and gullies, with sections of easy rock climbing. The final stretch of the couloir narrows and holds a finger of perennial snow. About 300 feet below the top of the couloir, work up and right on moderate rock (or snow) to the right side of the summit area. A short scramble westward brings one to

Kicking steps up the main couloir below The Worshipper

the tiny exposed summit and into the very heart of the Tetons.

Aerial view from the southeast: Cascade Canyon, Storm Point, Symmetry Couloir, Symmetry Spire, and Hanging Canyon at right.

Cascade Canyon Crags

NORTHWEST ACROSS JENNY LAKE, a compelling group of crags thrusts up to form a jagged skyline above the mouth of Cascade Canyon. The highest of these, characterized by a double south buttress, is Symmetry Spire. The southernmost summit, the walls of which drop steeply into Cascade Canyon, is Storm Point. Ice Point is the smaller summit between the two. Cube Point is the first major pinnacle below the summit along the east ridge of Symmetry Spire. Near the bottom of the east ridge and on its south slope is the small but coveted Baxter Pinnacle.

In the Tetons, where approaches are sometimes more arduous than the routes to which they lead, any faintly interesting crag or peak with a short approach is going to be popular. The main routes on Storm Point, Symmetry Spire, Cube Point, and Baxter Pinnacle have for many years been the standard "crag climbs" in the range. These climbs are graced with beautiful rock, commanding vistas, and relatively uncomplicated descents. The approaches, which are trivial compared to those of the Grand Teton or Mount Moran, can be made still shorter by taking the tour boat across Jenny Lake. A boat departs about every thirty minutes (or less) and requires about 10 minutes to reach the mouth of Cascade Canyon. A round trip ticket costs about $4.00. Note that the last launch of the day returns at six in the evening.

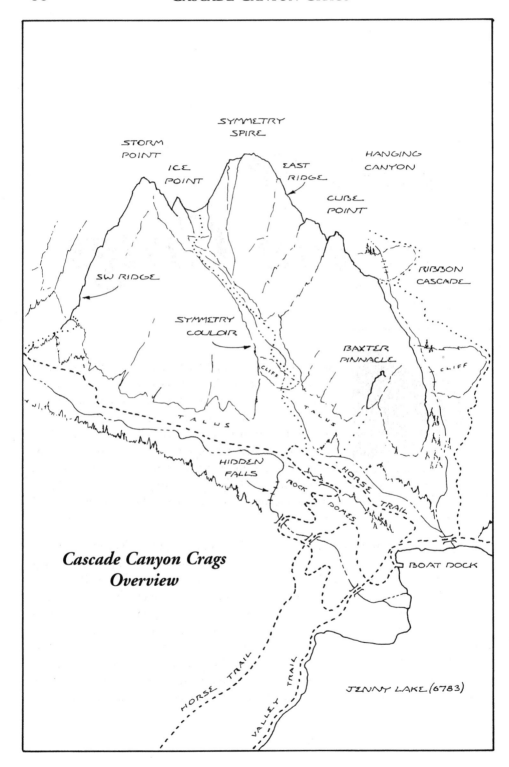

Cascade Canyon Crags Overview

Storm Point

Storm Point (10054) is the massive crag south of Symmetry Spire and across Cascade Canyon from Teewinot Mountain. Its pointed summit is readily visible from the east shore of Jenny Lake. Though many routes have been completed on this feature, it is interesting that Guide's Wall is the only one to have become popular or even known to most climbers.

35. *Guide's Wall*
III 8 to 10c

Guide's Wall is the name given to the first nine pitches of the Southwest Ridge route on Storm Point. The original line follows the entire 3000-foot ridge to the summit and requires about 40 pitches. Now, only the first six pitches are normally climbed. The Southwest Ridge first was ascended by Richard Pownall and Art Gilkey during the summer of 1949; more difficult variations have been developed over the years by different parties.

Approach. From the Jenny Lake ranger station, walk southwest a short way to the marina and catch a boat to the west shore of Jenny Lake. If travel by boat is ruled out, walk across the bridge immediately south of the marina and follow the trail 1.6 miles around the south side of Jenny Lake. From a trail junction near the west shore boat landing (see map), hike circa 1.8 miles up Cascade Canyon to where a rock slide has caused the formation of a large pond. The southwest ridge of Storm Point is directly north from the east end of the pond. Hike up the rock slide to the first cliffband, scramble right across a convenient ledge, follow a steep path up and right, then, go up to the west to the top of a ramp.

The Route. From the top of the ramp, scramble left behind a tree, go up a steeper ramp to a ledge on the west side of the arête, and set the belay.

1a.   Climb a right-facing dihedral with a fixed pin (7) and follow cracks and corners to a two-bolt anchor 15 feet above an obvious ledge (120 feet).

1b.   From behind the initial tree, climb the obvious roof (10a) and the clean dihedrals above to the two-bolt anchor.

2.   Climb an undistinguished pitch with harder variations to the right or left (7) and belay on a broad ledge with two trees (100 feet).

3a.   Climb a long, left-facing dihedral on the left side of the arête and belay at a stance at its top (7100 feet).

3b.   From the trees, move right along the ledge and belay at two boulders.

Now, climb a steep finger crack with pitons to a ledge (8), pull over a roof (7), and continue up easier terrain to a ledge with a small tree (100 feet).

4. From either option on pitch three, climb a short, easy pitch to Flake Ledge, a long terrace that wraps around the arête and is characterized by a 30-foot spike of rock.

5a. Climb twin cracks just right of the spike (7) and belay at a stance just past the roof (80 feet).

Fifth pitch variation, Guide's Wall

5b. Climb the exquisite handcrack a few feet to the right and merge left at the roof (9+). One also may crank through the roof at an obvious spike (10b/c).

5c. Begin to the left of the spike and tackle a right-facing flake/crack (10c).

6. Continue up a shallow dihedral and a thin crack with three fixed pins (8+), move left on a ledge and belay from a two-bolt anchor.

Descent. Make the first of four long rappels from the bolt anchor at the top of the sixth pitch. Note that the second and third rappels are from trees and that a short traverse southward along a ledge is required to reach the final bolt anchor 150 feet above the start of the climb.

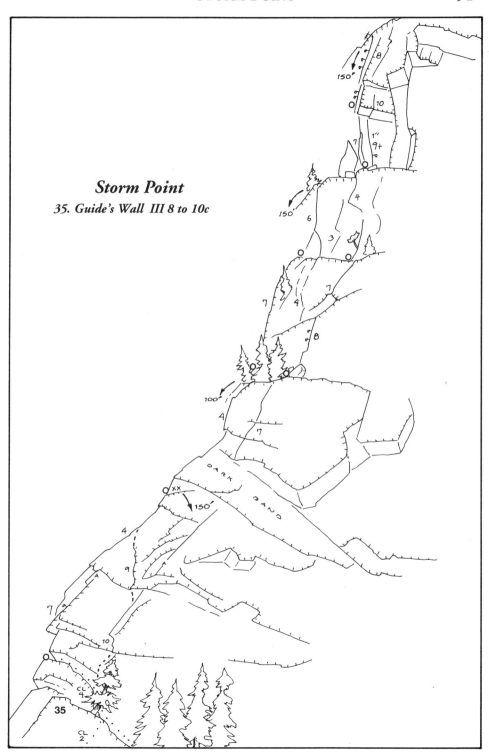

Storm Point

35. Guide's Wall III 8 to 10c

Storm Point, Ice Point, Symmetry Couloir, and Symmetry Spire
above Jenny Lake

Ice Point

36. Northwest Ridge
I Class 4

Ice Point (9920+) is the beautiful little spire along the ridge between Storm Point and Symmetry Spire. Its north shoulder forms the south side of Symmetry Col. Approach via the Symmetry Couloir (see below). To reach the summit from the col, follow the ridgecrest south staying a bit on the east side. Gain a notch in the steeper west ridge and follow the narrow crest to the summit. The first ascent was made by Fritiof Fryxell and Frank Smith on 13 August 1931. From the notch in the ridge, one may traverse south and scramble to the summit of Storm Point (cl3).

Symmetry Spire

Symmetry Spire (10560+) is the highest feature in the group of summits at the east end of the divide between Cascade Canyon and Hanging Canyon. It may be recognized from the southeast by its double south buttress. Though its approaches are more arduous than those to Storm Point or Baxter Pinnacle, the climbing is superb and the Southwest Ridge route is one of the best moderate rock climbs in the Tetons.

Approach A. The standard approach ascends the Symmetry Couloir, the big gully that climbs to the west between Storm Point and Symmetry Spire. Take the boat across Jenny Lake or hike around the lake from the marina or from the String Lake parking area. A short way north of the west shore boat dock, a "horse trail" branches west. Hike this trail through forests and beneath Baxter Pinnacle to where it levels out and crosses an alluvial fan with a small stream. Here a climber's path follows the drainage up brushy talus to a cliffband that blocks access to the Symmetry Couloir. Pass the cliff at right, then traverse up and left above the cliff until a faint path leads up and right to the north side of the couloir. After 100 feet or more, the path works back to the south side. Continue in this line to an upper cliffband which is passed along its south side. Scramble up and right to Symmetry Col (the saddle between Ice Point and Symmetry Spire) or work right to one of the routes on Symmetry Spire. An ice axe and boots suitable for kicking steps in snow are needed until mid to late summer when most of the couloir is free of snow.

Approach B. Symmetry Spire may be approached from the north via Hanging Canyon which also is the approach to Cube Point. Hike the lakeshore trail as noted above and reach a clearing where the trail crosses the drainage from Hanging Canyon. Locate a large dead spruce tree with the top blown off and its roots across the main trail. Just east of this tree, a footpath climbs up the slope into Hanging Canyon. The trail passes an initial cliffband on the right, then continues to a second steep area beneath Cube Point. The waterfall here is called Ribbon Cascade. Pass this section most easily on the right and continue to Arrowhead Pool on a bench above Ribbon Cascade. Easy hiking then leads to Ramshead Lake beneath the north face of Symmetry Spire.

Descent. From the summit, downclimb the Northwest Ledges (cl4) to Col 10300 (on the west side of the peak), then continue down the Southwest Couloir or the Northwest Couloir (below). It also is possible to rappel 75 feet west into the Southwest Couloir from a gap in the ridge below the last steep section along the crest of the Southwest Ridge; look for a sling anchor.

37. Southwest Couloir
II Class 4

This route provides an easy method of reaching the summit as well as the usual line of descent on the south side. From Symmetry Col at the top of the Symmetry Couloir, hike north on snow or scree and ascend the steep couloir at the western margin of Symmetry Spire for about 600 feet to its top at Col 10300. Scramble east up the ridge for about 100 feet, then follow ledges out onto the upper north face. From here a path zigzags up ledges to the summit. The section above the col is the old Northwest Ledges route.

38. Southwest Ridge
II 7

The southwest ridge rises steeply, without interruption to the right of the Southwest Couloir and poses one of the best moderate rock climbs in the Tetons. This great route was established by Bert Jensen and Walter Spofford on 30 July 1938.

The Route. Begin at the bottom of the ridge among some small trees or about 100 feet up to the left.

1. and 2. Climb steep but moderate rock for two pitches and gain a broken ledge system in dark rock beneath a steep wall with several right-facing dihedrals (4). Belay on the highest ledge at right.

3a. Climb the third dihedral from the left straight up to a ledge (7,120 feet).

3b. Start up the third dihedral but traverse right into the next corner and climb to the same ledge (5).

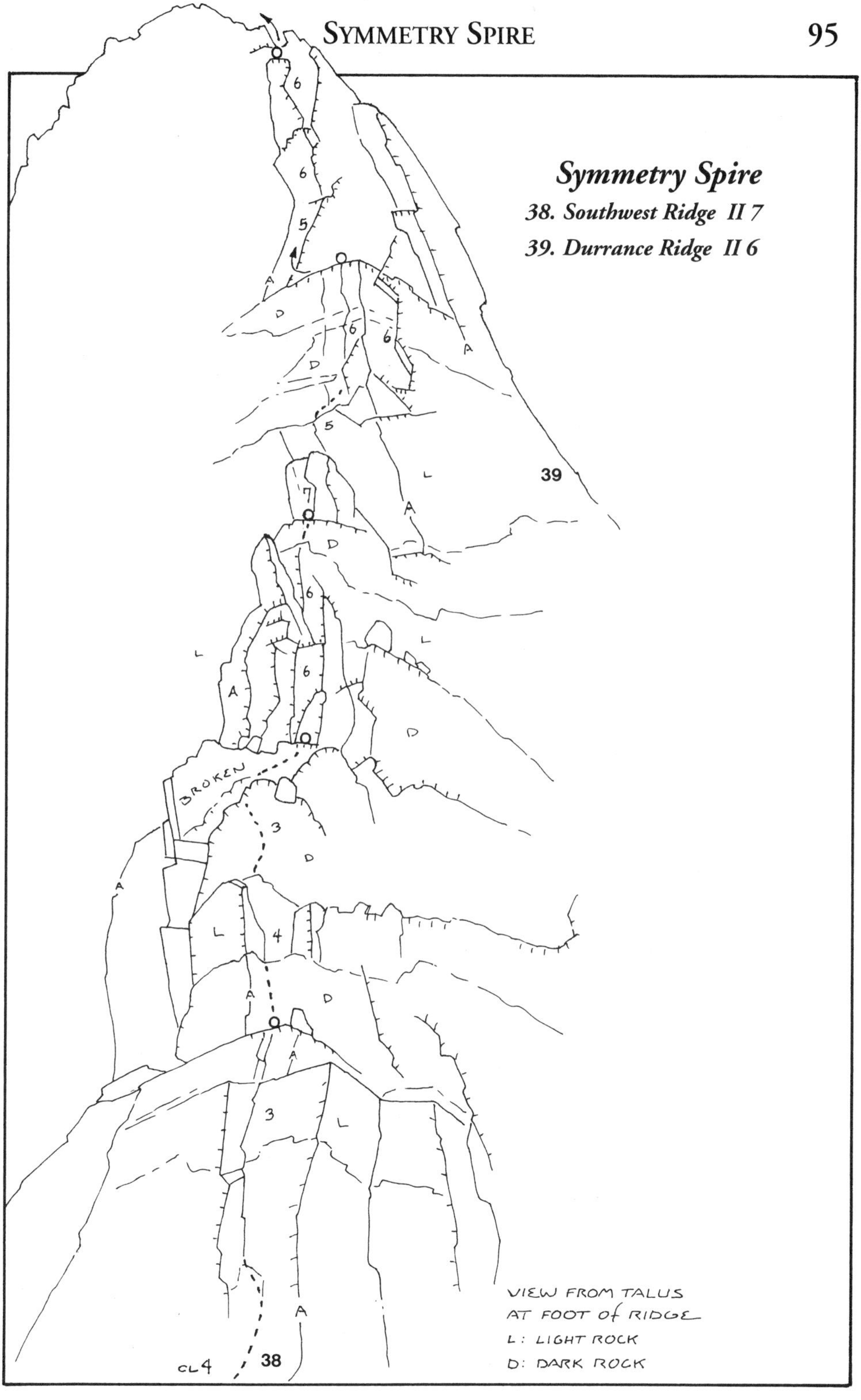

Symmetry Spire
38. Southwest Ridge II 7
39. Durrance Ridge II 6

39

6

6

5

A

D

6   6

A

D

5

7

D

L

A

6

L

D

6

L

A

6

D

BROKEN

3

A

D

L   4

A   D

A

3   L

A

VIEW FROM TALUS
AT FOOT OF RIDGE
L: LIGHT ROCK
D: DARK ROCK

CL 4   **38**

4. Climb straight up a "nose" of golden rock past some fixed pins and belay on a ledge (7) or run the rope out to the next belay. The "nose" can be avoided by traversing around it on the right.

5a. From the belay above the "nose," climb straight up dark rock to the left of the crest and belay on a big ledge (5).

5b. From the top of the "nose," work up and right to the crest and follow a shallow corner on the right to the big ledge.

6. Step down to the left and climb a steep ramp that angles up and right (5). Belay at its top or continue up through the next pitch.

7. Climb a steep face of dark rock and negotiate a steep flake either by climbing the chimney along its right side or the face at left (6). Belay atop the flake.

Cross to the right side of the ridge and follow the crest to the summit.

39. Durrance Ridge
II 6

Several hundred feet to the east of the southwest ridge, a deep couloir known as Templeton's Crack splits the south face of Symmetry Spire; the long ridge that forms the left side of this couloir is called the Durrance Ridge. This is an easier climb than the Southwest Ridge that features excellent, steep rock with good protection and good belays. There are ten pitches of climbing. Jack Durrance and Walter Spofford made the first ascent on 7 August 1936.

The Route. Begin at the very foot of the ridge, adjacent to Templeton's Crack. Climb several moderate pitches on the crest of the ridge to a steep 25-foot wall about halfway up. Climb a crack with a fixed pin (5) to pass the wall, then continue on easier ground for about 200 feet (cl4) to where the angle steepens. A final consideration remains to be reckoned: Just left of the crest of the ridge, climb a long crack system with some fixed pins (6) and a short chimney that leads to the top of the ridge. Beware of a loose chockstone on this pitch. Now, climb up and left (west) to the upper Southwest Ridge and follow the crest to the summit.

40. Direct Jensen Ridge
III 8

The Jensen Ridge forms the right (east) side of Templeton's Crack and is considerably more difficult than the Southwest Ridge route, however, the middle section of the climb degenerates into steep scrambling on less than wonderful rock. The route was pieced together by different parties between 1938 and 1953; the first free ascent of the entire ridge was completed by Willi Unsoeld, Mary Sylvander, and Steve Jervis on 16 August 1953.

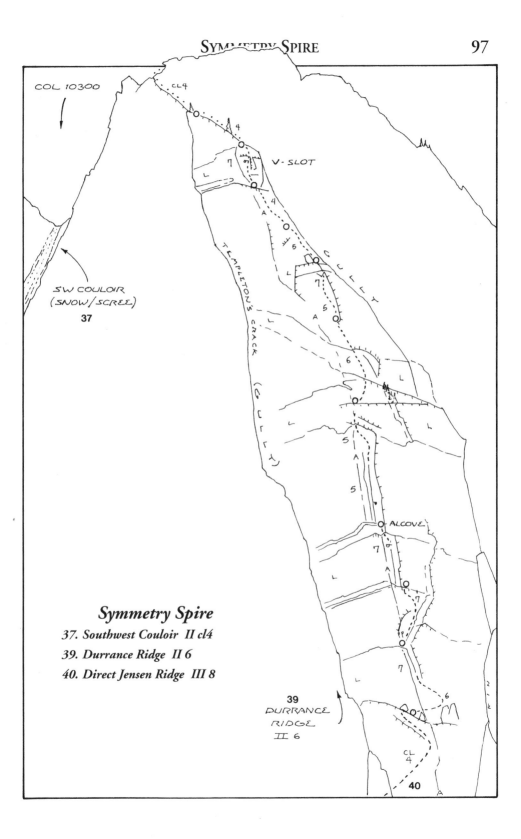

COL 10300

CL4

V-SLOT

SW COULOIR
(SNOW/SCREE)

37

TEMPLETON'S CRACK (GULLY)

GULLY

ALCOVE

Symmetry Spire

37. Southwest Couloir II cl4

39. Durrance Ridge II 6

40. Direct Jensen Ridge III 8

39
DURRANCE
RIDGE
II 6

CL
4

40

The Route. From the bottom of the Durrance Ridge, descend into Templeton's Crack and traverse east onto the ridge. Traverse right to within 50 feet of the gully on the right side of the ridge, then work up and left to belay on a ledge.

1. Traverse right to some flakes, then cut back left to a vertical crack which is climbed to a ledge beneath a large overhang (7).

2. Work up under the roof, traverse right over the top of a large flake, then work up and left to belay on a ledge beside a left-facing dihedral. Move the belay to the corner of the dihedral.

3. Climb up toward a flake, then move back right and go straight up to the top of the dihedral (8). Belay in a deep alcove.

4. The next pitch may be climbed on either side of the crest. The left version ascends cracks in the left wall of a large dihedral (5). Exit the dihedral in a chimney, work up the face, and belay on a long ledge halfway up the ridge.

5. Climb steep slabs and belay at the bottom of a left-facing dihedral (6).

6. Climb slabs out and left from the dihedral, then veer back to the right and climb through a slot (7) to a good ledge.

7. Climb an easy lead up and slightly right to a stance on the crest (5).

8. Scramble up and left for a ropelength or more and belay on a ledge left of the crest (4).

9. Work up and slightly left and climb an awkward V-slot through a roof (7+). Belay above where the angle eases off.

10. Climb a long moderate pitch that passes a small roof on the right (4).

Scramble up to the west and intersect the final section of the Southwest Ridge route. Scramble to the summit or rappel 75 feet west from the notch in the ridge.

41. East Ridge
II Class 4

The first ascent of Symmetry Spire was made via the east ridge on 20 August 1929 by Fritiof Fryxell and Phil Smith. This highly visible ridge provides an excellent climb. It also may be used as a descent from the summit to avoid snow in the northeast couloir. Approach via Hanging Canyon (see above) and hike to Arrowhead Pool above Ribbon Cascade. Cross the stream west of the pool and gain a grassy shelf that leads out onto the east ridge. The minor summit on the ridge just east of this point is called Sam's Tower. Follow the ridge about 1000 feet to the summit.

Richard Rossiter on the dihedral pitch, Southwest Ridge, 1975

Cube Point as seen from Hanging Canyon

42. Northwest Couloir
I Class 4

From the isthmus between Ramshead Lake and Lake of the Crags, hike north and continue up the steep couloir on snow or scree to Col 10300 between Symmetry Spire and Symmetry Crags to the west. From here one may climb the Northwest Ledges (cl4) to the summit or descend the Southwest Couloir to routes on the south side. All of this makes more sense if a high camp is established in Hanging Canyon, which is a great way to hang out for a few days (pun intended) and bag some routes. The Northwest Couloir also may be used in conjunction with the Hanging Canyon waytrail as an alternate descent to avoid snow in the standard Southwest Couloir-Symmetry Couloir descent.

Cube Point

Cube Point (9600+) is the prominent tooth-like summit on the long east ridge that descends from Symmetry Spire. The smaller summit just to the west is Sam's Tower. Cube Point takes its name from a large, angular block that forms the actual summit. Approach via Hanging Canyon (see Approach II under Symmetry Spire). To descend from the summit, downclimb the East Couloir route or rappel from a tree to the col on the west side.

43. East Couloir
II Class 4

This is the easiest route to the summit but it is more often used to reach the East Ridge; it also is the usual choice for descent. In early season it is a good snow climb. The first ascent is uncertain. From the bench below and immediately east of Ribbon Falls, hike southwest up a talus fan and enter the couloir that curves up around the east ridge of Cube Point. Follow the couloir around to the south side of the tower and climb to its end at a small notch. Turn north and gain the crest. The final block may be ascended by it south or west side.

44. East Ridge
II 4

The East Ridge route on Cube Point is a Teton mini-classic. It is often used as an early season warm-up featuring a sweeping snow couloir and excellent rock. The first ascent is uncertain. Follow the East Couloir (above) to where it narrows and curves around the bottom of the east ridge. Leave the snow and climb the ridge to a big ledge (cl4). Climb a steep but well-protected pitch up excellent rock on the crest to where the angle eases off. Continue up the ridge to the almost level summit crest and scramble to the "cube" which is ascended by its south or west side.

Baxter Pinnacle

There are very few "short subjects" in the Tetons, that is, compact rock climbs with easy access. Among such leisurely outings, Baxter Pinnacle (8560+) is as short as they get. A 30 minute approach leads to five pitches of good rock with a sunny southern exposure and pleasant vista above Jenny Lake. The pinnacle can be seen from the east shore of the lake, low on the south side of Symmetry Spire's east ridge but it is difficult to discern. The complete South Ridge route as described below was first climbed by Barry Corbet and Robert French on 27 July 1958.

Approach. Take the boat across Jenny Lake or walk around as described under Approach A for Symmetry Spire. In either case, from a trail junction a short way west of the boat landing, take the "horse trail" up Cascade Canyon. After about a half mile, Baxter Pinnacle can be seen on the slope to the north. Continue up the trail to where it crosses the talus field that descends from the pinnacle. Here, a foot-path leads up to the base of the south ridge.

45. South Ridge
II 9+

To begin, scramble up a gully, first on the east side of the ridge, then back toward the crest. Belay above a large block.

1. Work up and left along a ramp, then go back right past a tree and belay on a ledge where the terrain steepens. One also may climb straight up a steep wall with two bolts to reach the second belay (10); this steep variation is called Seizure Disorder.

2. Climb a steep crack with fixed pins to the right of the crest (8) or ascend an easier system just left of this and belay on the ridge crest.

3. Climb directly up the crest (6), finishing the pitch with a steep hand-crack (6) or climb a chimney to the right (6).

4. In either case, an easier pitch brings one to the base of the intimidating summit tower.

5. Here, the route follows a steep crack and corner system up and left across the south face. Climb a bit to the right past a fixed pin (9+) and up to a large, detached flake (optional belay). Now, lieback up and left along a very steep corner with fixed pins and up double cracks to the summit (7).

To descend from the summit, rappel 75 feet into the notch to the north, then downclimb the steep couloir along the west side of the pinnacle. Be very careful of loose rock on the climb as well as the descent.

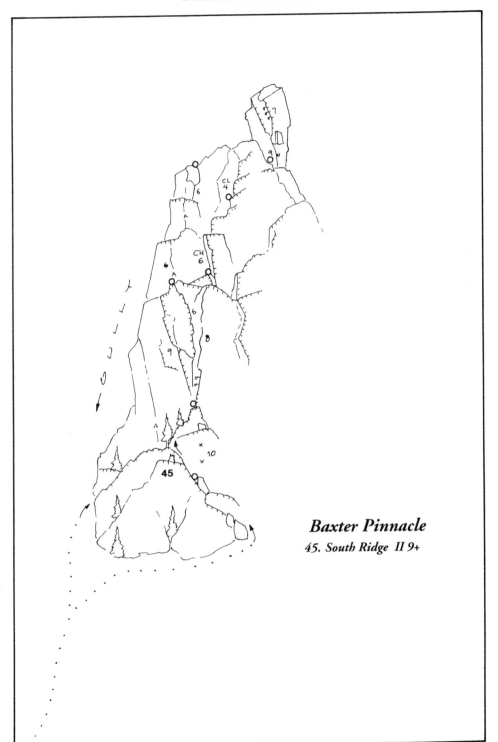

Baxter Pinnacle
45. South Ridge II 9+

Aerial view of Mount Moran from the southeast

Mount Moran

MOUNT MORAN (12605) is the northern monarch of the Teton Range. Though the Grand Teton is higher and draws a good deal more attention, it cannot match the massive bulk and complexity of this awesome peak. That it sees relatively few ascents is due not only to its lesser height but to the fact that no maintained trail leads to any of its routes. Rising from the shores of both Leigh Lake and Jackson Lake, its summit presents an elevation gain of 5728 feet - a respectable day's jaunt by any standard.

The earliest known attempt on the summit was made by LeRoy Jeffers who on 11 August 1919 climbed the Skillet Glacier to the false summit of the northeast ridge. He would no doubt have continued to the main summit but for darkness and bad weather. He returned 6 August 1922 with W.H. Loyster but upon reaching the main summit found evidence that the peak had been climbed via the same route just ten days earlier by LeGrand Hardy, Ben C. Rich, and Bennet McNulty.

The sprawling ramparts of Mount Moran are sufficiently complex to render a verbal description both protracted and bewildering (not to mention boring). Fortunately, all the routes cataloged here can be approached from the String Lake picnic area and ascend adjacent aspects of the mountain. Thus, our survey of terrain features may be kept thankfully brief.

Viewing the mountain from the southeast it will be useful to identify the following features: Immediately southwest of Mount Moran, and connected to it by a high ridge, is Thor Peak (12028). Down to the right (east) of Thor Peak, the massive south buttress of Moran towers over Leigh Canyon; above, the south ridge continues to the summit. To the right of the south buttress is the cirque of the Laughing Lion Snowfield from which a deep couloir descends into Leigh Canyon. Laughing

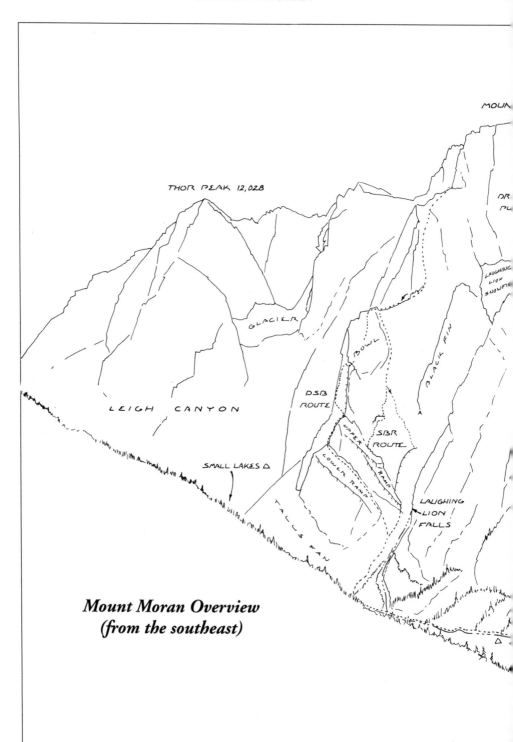

THOR PEAK 12,028

MOUN

DR
PU

LAUGHING
LION
SNOWFIE

GLACIER

BOWL

BLACK FIN

LEIGH CANYON

DSB
ROUTE

SBR
ROUTE

UPPER RAMP

LOWER RAMP

SMALL LAKES △

TALUS FAN

LAUGHING
LION
FALLS

△

**Mount Moran Overview
(from the southeast)**

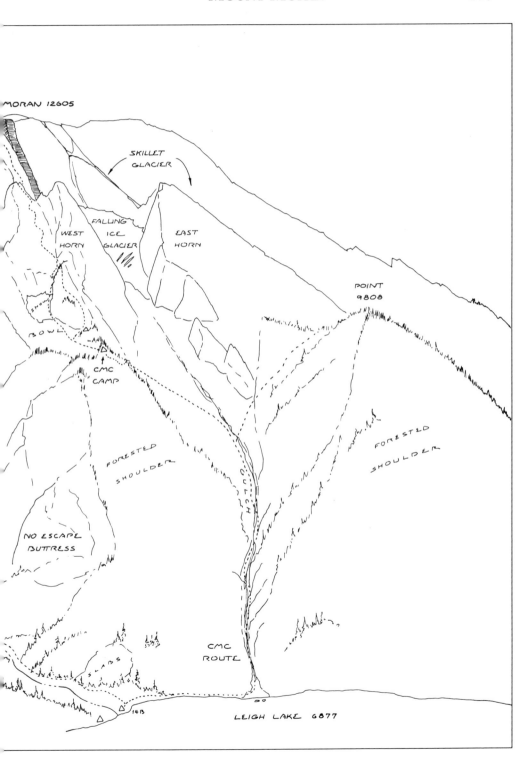

Lion Falls, perhaps the hardest winter ice climb in Wyoming, is located in this gully. To the east of the gully, the narrow Staircase Arete climbs steeply to the southeast ridge which continues to the summit of Drizzlepuss, a clandestine tower along the CMC Route. Around to the right from the southeast flank of the mountain, a long drainage descends from the Falling Ice Glacier which is flanked by two giant towers, the West Horn and East Horn. Above the glacier, the CMC Face and the Black Dike climb to the broad summit plateau. Not visible from the southeast, the Skillet Glacier occupies the cirque north of the East Horn.

On the west face of Drizzlepuss

General Approach. By far, the easiest way to reach the southeast side of Mount Moran is by canoe. Make the initial launch at the String Lake picnic area and paddle to the north end of the lake where a sign marks the beginning of a 300 yard portage. A fifteen minute deltoid workout brings one to the south shore of Leigh Lake. Paddle to the mouth of Leigh Canyon at the extreme west end of the lake. If expeditious, the entire approach via canoe requires about 90 minutes.

If approach by canoe is ruled out (and you had better have a good reason), begin from the parking area at String Lake, shoulder thy burden, and hike the Valley Trail 3.5 miles to the north end of Leigh Lake. From here, labor westward along a primitive trail that follows the shoreline to the cascade that descends from the Falling Ice Glacier. A good initial campsite lies a short way west at the mouth of Leigh Canyon (permit required). For those incurably bent on self abuse, this area also may be reached by a devastating bushwhack along the southwest shore of Leigh Lake.

Descent. From the summit, the easiest descent probably is to downclimb the CMC Route, which involves about 1000 feet of steep, exposed slabs on the CMC Face. Most parties will want to make at least two rappels on this section, the first from slings above Unsoeld's Needle and the second from a stance on the needle's east side (see topo). It also is necessary to climb the steep west face of Drizzlepuss (4) beyond which a numbing 4700 feet of steep scree and short cliffs lead ever downward to Leigh Lake. Very careful routefinding is necessary on this descent if it is being done for the first time. See CMC Route below. It also is possible to descend the Skillet Glacier but this requires an ice axe, mountain boots, crampons, and well developed skills in steep snow travel.

46. Direct South Buttress
IV 7 A3 or 12a

In every mountain range there are a few routes that, due to their length, position, quality, and history, are recognized as the great classic lines. The Direct South Buttress on Mount Moran is a route of such stature and, at the time of its first ascent, was the hardest climb in the Tetons. The "Direct" combines difficult aid and free climbing on the very prow of the south buttress, then continues more easily up the long, rugged south ridge to the summit. The route was first climbed on 29 and 30 August 1953 by Richard Emerson, Don Decker, and Leigh Ortenburger. Rack up to a #4 Friend.

Approach. Reach the designated campsites at the mouth of Leigh Canyon as described above. Camp here or proceed approximately 0.5 mile up the canyon to a point directly south of the west arête of No Return Buttress; find a good campsite in a stand of trees on the south side of the stream. It also is possible, though perhaps less convenient, to camp at two small lakes about 1.5 miles up the canyon.

There are several paths leading out of the lakeside campsites and taking the wrong one in the wee hours of the morning would be a disastrous affair, as lower Leigh Canyon is a maze of fallen trees, bogs, and dense undergrowth. The correct path begins from the east edge of campsite 14b. After a few feet, a right branch leads along the lake to the CMC route, so bear left. The path is sinuous and sometimes indistinct but, for the most part, stays in the bottom of the valley, always on the north side of the stream.

After about three-quarters of a mile, the path fades and one breaks out of the woods. Continue along the bank of the stream until below a gully that descends from an unlikely waterfall up on the peak (Laughing Lion Falls). The Staircase Arete climbs to the right of the falls, to the left is the massive south buttress. The "Direct" lies just beyond the prow on the western skyline. The hanging plane of the South Buttress Right is discernible about midway between the prow and Laughing Lion Falls. Note also two long ramps that angle up to the west across the bottom of the buttress. Hike up the talus slope west of the gully that descends from Laughing Lion Falls, then scramble all the way to the western end of the lower ramp. A bivouac can be made here.

The Route. Rope up about 50 feet around to the left of the prow, between two trees.

1. and 2. Climb a chimney system for 200 feet and belay at the top of the upper ramp (cl4).

3. Move the belay about 50 feet to the west. Work up and right, then back left to a long ledge systems that curves up to the left (7).

4. Scramble up and left along the ledge for 165 feet (4).

5. Climb up and left past fixed pins and belay on a ramp (8).

6. From the ramp, climb up and right past a flake, then straight up a right-facing dihedral to a roof. Handtraverse left (9) and belay at a large flake. Note that there are easier alternatives to these pitches to the left (see topo).

7. Climb a left-facing dihedral, then work up the clean chimney formed by a long detached flake and belay at its top (7).

8. Climb up to the left side of a huge, white-topped flake, lieback up around its left side, then work up past a thin, pointed flake to a ledge (7).

9. Work up and right to a ledge with a fixed pin, move to the right around a blunt arête, and climb a steep crack up to a tiny ledge beneath two bolts (8).

10. This is the famous double pendulum pitch. Climb up to the bolts, lower 20 feet, then pendulum to a wafer piton. Lower down again and swing across to a small stance below a thin crack (optional belay). Aid (A1) or free climb (12a) up and right past fixed pins to a good ledge and belay. It is possible to avoid the pendulums by traversing straight across the face at the level of the optional belay (11d).

11. Handtraverse to the right along a good flake and, after about 100 feet, belay on a ledge at the bottom of a huge bowl (5). If a bivouac is required, scramble up and right across the bowl to a thicket of small pine trees. Water may be found here in early to mid season.

To continue to the summit, climb along the left edge of the bowl, gain the crest of the south ridge, and traverse a level section for 1000 feet to the next steep step in the ridge. There are several pinnacles along this section, the last of which may require a 60-foot rappel. Pass a notch (see descent), traverse a bit to the right and ascend the ridge staying mostly on the east side of the crest. The final steep section before the summit is most easily negotiated on the west side. The entire ridge above the south buttress can be climbed unroped by a competent team and, if the easiest line is found, the difficulty does not exceed 4.

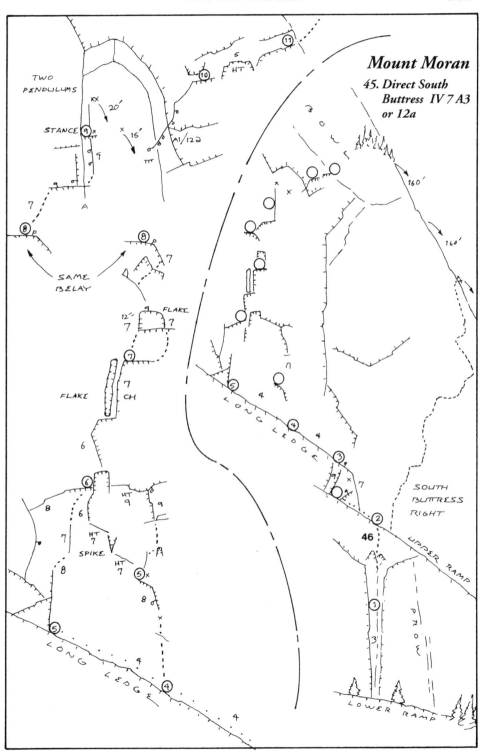

Mount Moran
45. Direct South Buttress IV 7 A3 or 12a

To avoid the upper 3000 feet of the south ridge and return to Leigh Canyon:

Descent A. Scramble up to the notch at the north end of the level section of the south ridge as described above. From here, two steep gullies divided by a rock rib drop down to the west. Downclimb the left gully for about 250 feet, then CHANGE TO THE RIGHT (more northerly) gully and follow it down into the basin between Thor Peak and the south ridge. This is no piece of cake but can be managed without rappels.

Descent B. An alternate descent involving about ten long rappels can be made from the trees up and right across the bowl from the top of the eleventh pitch. From the lowest of these trees, make two long rappels to reach the top of the rappel route for South Buttress Right (see topo).

47. South Buttress Right
IV 11a

From the southeast shore of Leigh Lake, the great south buttress of Mount Moran rises on the left in silhouette against Thor Peak; its nearly vertical western prow is ascended by the Direct South Buttress route. About 500 feet down to the east across the broad south face of the buttress (roughly midway), a series of huge right-facing dihedrals and overhangs angles up and right in dramatic stages to merge with the blunt ridge on the east. The South Buttress Right, widely considered the finest rock climb in the Tetons, ascends a narrow plane of rock that literally hangs in space between two immense corner and roof systems. This is a very steep route with ever engaging climbing on solid, fine-grained granite. The exposure is from a different reality.

The route first was climbed on 25 July 1961 by Dave Dornan and Herb Swedlund. The first complete free ascent of the original line was made on 2 August 1978 by Buck Tilley and Jim Mullin. Rack up to a #3 Friend with relatively few RPs and stoppers. Two of the smallest TCUs or quarter-inch pitons can be used at the crux (pitch three).

Approach. Follow the approach for the Direct South Buttress to the talus field beneath the two diagonal ramps, then hike to the highest ledge beneath the east end of the upper ramp, just left of Laughing Lion Falls.

The Route. Climb a grungy chimney (8) or a clean crack to the right (8, 4 inches) followed by a short right-facing corner. This brings one to the east end of the upper ramp. Now, unrope and scramble up the ramp for about 600 feet to the bottom of a long right-facing dihedral system. The first pitch may be identified by a large boulder at its base and a pointed block about 15 feet up in a small dihedral. There are three options for starting this pitch:

1a. Climb the face directly above the boulder and move right around the pointed block to gain the corner (8).

Aerial view from the southeast of the south buttress of Mount Moran

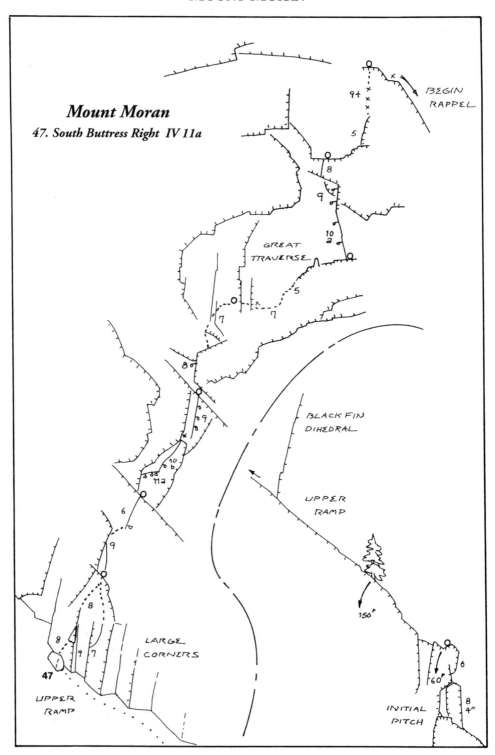

Mount Moran
47. South Buttress Right IV 11a

BEGIN RAPPEL

9+

5

8

9

10 a

GREAT TRAVERSE

5

7   7

8

9

BLACK FIN DIHEDRAL

10 b

11a

UPPER RAMP

6

9

150'

8

LARGE CORNERS

8

9   7

47

UPPER RAMP

60'

6

INITIAL PITCH

8 4"

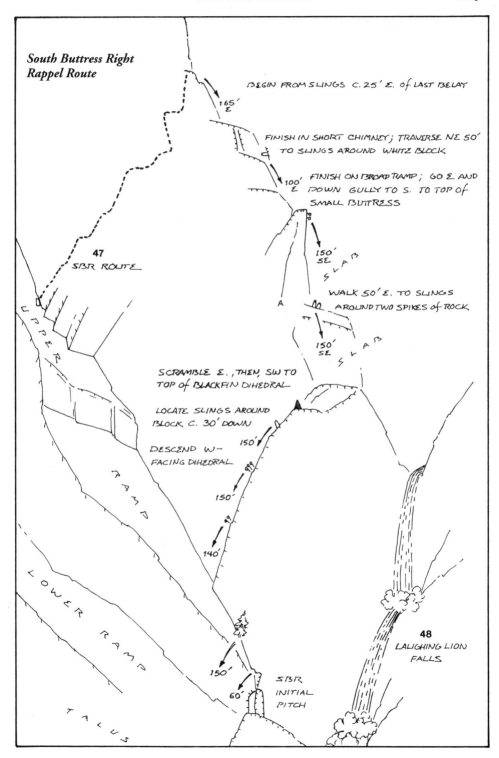

South Buttress Right Rappel Route

BEGIN FROM SLINGS C. 25' E. OF LAST BELAY

165'
E

FINISH IN SHORT CHIMNEY; TRAVERSE NE 50' TO SLINGS AROUND WHITE BLOCK

100'
E

FINISH ON BROAD RAMP; GO E. AND DOWN GULLY TO S. TO TOP OF SMALL BUTTRESS

150'
SE

S L A B

47
SBR ROUTE

WALK 50' E. TO SLINGS AROUND TWO SPIKES OF ROCK

A

150'
SE

S L A B

U P P E R

SCRAMBLE E., THEN, SW TO TOP OF BLACKFIN DIHEDRAL

LOCATE SLINGS AROUND BLOCK C. 30' DOWN

150'

DESCEND W— FACING DIHEDRAL

R A M P

150'

140'

L O W E R   R A M P

150'

60'

SBR INITIAL PITCH

48
LAUGHING LION FALLS

T A L U S

1b. Climb a finger crack in a right-facing dihedral about 12 feet east of the boulder (9).

1c. Climb a shallow left-facing corner and crack about 20 feet east of the boulder (7).

All versions merge; follow an easy crack to a ledge (90 feet). Beware of loose exfoliation about halfway up.

2. Climb a right-facing dihedral with a tricky lieback (9), then jam an easy crack on the right to a large ramp that slopes down to the east (100 feet).

3. Work up into a large right-facing dihedral with some fixed pins, make a desperate undercling out to the right (11a, smallest TCUs), and crank

Joyce Rossiter beginning the third pitch, South Buttress Right

around the corner to a "thank God" fixed pin. Lieback up the dihedral to a stance with a bolt (10b, optional belay), and finish with a thin crack (9, three pins) that leads to a sloping belay ledge (100 feet).

4. Climb a left-facing corner and roof just above the belay to a ledge (8), pull up past a flake, then work right along an easy hand traverse to an exposed, marginal stance at the near side of a right-facing corner (100 feet). Before the hand traverse, a tempting crack goes straight up to what appears to be another ledge; this is off-route.

5. To the east of the belay, an immense slab hangs above empty space. There are some narrow ledges at the far side. Your mission, should you choose to accept it, is to reach these ledges. This is the Great Traverse. Move right past the dihedral to a fixed pin (or sling a horn 20 feet above), then continue east across the slab (7, no pro) and gain a series of flakes that lead up to the ledges. Belay at the far right beneath an obvious, left-angling handcrack (150 feet).

6. Lieback and jam the crack (10a), work up and left through a V-shaped break in the roof (9), and belay on a large, grassy ledge (150 feet).

7. Move the belay to the east end of the ledge. Climb a left-facing flake/corner and the smooth face above past four antique bolts (9+, 90 feet). Belay on a big ledge.

Options: 25 feet down to the east, a cluster of slings marks the beginning of the rappel route back to the start of the climb (see rappel topo). It also is possible to climb several more pitches up and left to join the Direct South Buttress route at the long, level stretch in the ridge. After the first two or three pitches, a bivouac can be made in a thicket of trees as described for that route.

48. Laughing Lion Falls
IV 9 A3 WI4

To see Laughing Lion Falls in the summer, one cannot help speculate what manner of mind altering ascent it would provide when frozen in the deep of winter. The six-pitch route was attempted seven or eight times before it was climbed successfully by Jack Tackle, Alex Lowe, and Andy Carson during the winter of 1987. Bring the usual ice climbing gear plus a rock climbing rack and a selection of pitons. The amount and thickness of the ice varies greatly from year to year. Approach as for South Buttress Right (above). To descend from the top of the last pitch, rappel the route.

The Route.

1. WI3, 120 feet. The ice may be thin and separated from the rock.

2. WI3, 150 feet.

3. WI2, 80 feet.

Slog up through snow for about 700 feet.

4. Climb a chimney that may or may not be filled with ice (6).

5. Continue up rock and turn a roof or bulge (9, A3); this pitch was considered the crux on the first ascent.

6. WI4, 150 feet. A final pitch of good, steep ice leads to the top of the climb.

49. CMC Route
III 4 or 6

This direct line on the southeast aspect of the mountain is the most popular summit route and is the one most often used for descent. Perhaps not ironically, its first ascent by Paul Petzoldt, Joseph Hawkes, Earl Clark, and Harold Plumely of the Chicago Mountaineering Club, came six years after it was first descended by Chris Scoredos and Joe Merhar on 14 July 1935. The latter two had made the second ascent of the South Ridge. The CMC Route features minimal bushwhacking, sound rock, tremendous relief, and a splendid campsite with water at 10,000 feet. The entire ascent may be managed unroped by a competent cragster but bear in mind that some steep and tricky downclimbing will be required. Most parties will want to belay and rappel the steeper sections of the route.

Approach. Make camp at the mouth of Leigh Canyon (see General Approach above). From campsite 14b, a footpath leads north along the shore for about 400 yards to the stream that descends from the Falling Ice Glacier. From other camp-sites a short canoe ride will be highly useful in reaching this point. An alternative is to canoe directly to the Falling Ice Glacier drainage and trek up to the CMC camp the day before the climb (see below).

The Route. Begin from the lakeshore and ascend the rocky stream gully that leads to the Falling Ice Glacier. Switch banks as needed and follow a faint trail along the stream to the 9000-foot level. Now contour around to the southwest for some 200 yards and pick up a distinct trail that climbs a steep, grassy slope onto a wooded ridge. After a few switchbacks the trail leads straight up the ridge to the CMC camp at 10,000 feet. This site is easily identified by four or five manmade enclosures in a narrow stand of pine trees. Water may be found in the boulderfield about 100 feet to the south.

The next objective is to reach the summit of Drizzlepuss.

A. Perhaps the easiest of two alternatives is to hike west-northwest up the broad, open gully directly above the spring at the CMC camp. This may require mountain boots and an ice axe until August. Bear right near the top of the cirque and pick up a faint trail that leads to the talus field below the West Horn. Note a cairn near the highest trees on the right (east).

B. In early to mid-season, one may avoid the snow gully by hiking directly up the ridge above the CMC camp to a bench with a few more tent enclosures. Climb an easy chimney through the cliffband above the bench and pick up a faint path that meanders up the steep, wooded ridge. With careful navigation this will bring one to the cairn at the highest trees just south of the West Horn (see above). From the cairn, follow a faint north-west up loose scree to the col between the West Horn and Drizzlepuss, then scramble without difficulty to the summit of the latter.

From the summit of Drizzlepuss, the CMC Face comes into full view and there is the opportunity to examine the final 1000 feet of the route. The narrow spire just across the gap to the west is Unsoeld's Needle. Downclimb (4) or rappel the steep west face of Drizzlepuss into the narrow notch at its base. Rope up. Ascend a left-facing dihedral on Unsoeld's Needle for about 50 feet (4) to a piton anchor, then make a 150-foot horizontal traverse to the right out onto the CMC Face. Work up

Near the top of the CMC Route with the West Horn in the background

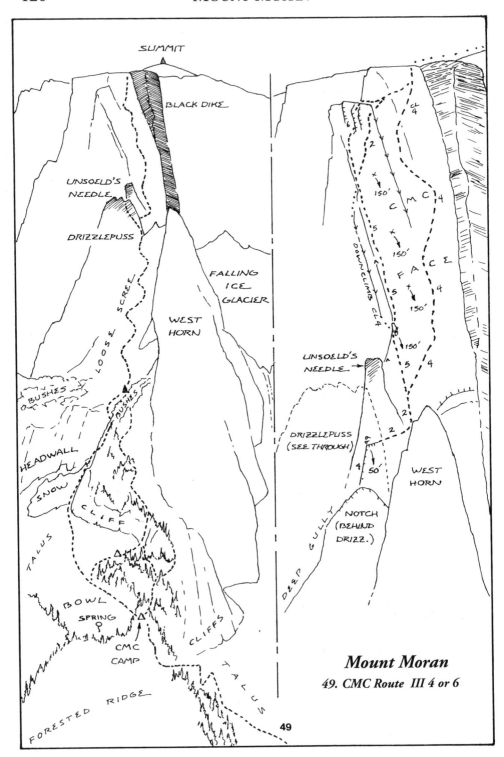

Mount Moran
49. CMC Route III 4 or 6

49

and left for about 100 feet toward the notch above Unsoeld's Needle, then work up and right into the middle of the broad face. Stay well left of the Black Dike and follow the line of least resistance to the summit plateau (see topo). The true summit is the huge mound of shattered sandstone (!) a short way north from the top of the Black Dike.

Arête Variation (6). A more difficult and perhaps more aesthetic variation continues up and left past Unsoeld's Needle to the arête at the left edge of the face (5). Follow the clean, exposed arête for several long pitches to near its very top (6), then traverse right for a couple of hundred feet and climb a short, steep dihedral with good protection (6). Continue to the right across the top of a deep gully (see Descent), then work up the final slabs and ledges of the regular route.

Descent. To descend from the summit one may simply reverse the route, however, the most expedient downclimb does not follow the usual line of ascent. Begin about 50 feet south of the Black Dike and climb down toward the West Horn via ramps and ledges (cl4). After about 300 feet, traverse south across the top of a deep gully and continue down and south to the very edge of the CMC face. Note that there is a rappel route about midway between the deep gully and south edge of the face that begins about 400 feet beneath the summit plateau. Two ropes are required. From the south edge of the face move around into a large south-facing corner system and descend another 400 feet until it is easy to work back left to a rappel station on the edge of the face. Rappel 165 feet or downclimb (5) the slab to the north of Unsoeld's Needle to an area of sloping ledges. Descend another 100 feet and make a 150-foot horizontal traverse to a small ledge at the southeast corner of the needle. Rappel 50 feet or downclimb (4) into the narrow notch between Unsoeld's Needle and Drizzlepuss.

Now it is necessary to climb the vertical but ledgey west face of Drizzlepuss. From the high point of the notch, descend about 20 feet to the south, then work up and right (4) along a ledge that leads out across the west face. At the first opportunity, move up to the next ledge, then continue more easily to the top of the tower. An alternative is to descend southward from the notch about 50 feet to an easier ledge that angles out into the middle of the face, then work up and left to join the other line. It also is possible to leave an extra rope through a rappel anchor about half-way up the west face so that the initial moves out of the notch (7 straight up) can be toproped on return from the summit.

From the top of Drizzlepuss, scramble southeast down snow or scree to two cairn on a shoulder with scrub trees to the south of the West Horn. The simplest venue is to descend a broad gully to the south, then hike down snow or talus east to the conspicuous wooded ridge of the CMC camp. A more difficult alternative is to reach the CMC camp by scrambling down a steep and erratic path that leads east from the cairn. This option is not recommended unless it was also the path of ascent. From the CMC camp, follow a distinct path down to the east, then north to gain the drainage from the Falling Ice Glacier which leads to the shore of Leigh Lake.

50. Skillet Glacier
III 4, steep snow or ice

Viewed from the east across Jackson Lake, the Skillet Glacier is easily identified by its shape which resembles, of course, a skillet with the handle pointing up toward the summit. The handle, that is, the narrow upper finger of the glacier breaches the 1500-foot eastern headwall of the peak and completes an unobstructed line of ascent from the shore of Jackson Lake to the summit plateau. This is a pure snow

Mount Moran from the east. The Skillet Glacier is down and right from the summit. Jackson Lake is at right.

and ice climb with a short section of slabby rock midway in the main glacier. Deft skills in snow and ice climbing are necessary, especially since the usual descent is to reverse the route; a slip from the steep upper couloir would be disastrous. In May and June, the Skillet Glacier offers a superb ski descent from the summit plateau to the shores of Jackson Lake, however, this should be attempted only by the expert alpine skier. The first ascent of this sweeping and conspicuous route was made by LeGrand Hardy, Ben C. Rich, and Bennet McNulty on 27 July 1922 which also was the first ascent of the mountain. Bring an ice axe, mountain boots, crampons, snow pickets, and a light rock climbing rack. In late season, ice screws are advisable.

Approach A. It is relatively easy to canoe from Coulter Bay Marina or Signal Mountain Campground about 2.3 miles (in either case) across Jackson Lake to the west shore of Bearpaw Bay below the Skillet Glacier. However, the easiest known method is as follows: Just west of North Jenny Lake Junction, turn north on a dirt road and drive to its end on the west shore Spalding Bay (Jackson Lake). Canoe north and west along the shoreline, then back south to the west shore of Bearpaw Bay for a total of 1.5 miles by canoe. A pleasant hike west through ancient forest and glacial moraine leads to the toe of glacier in 1.8 miles. A bivouac can be made in a thicket of trees just north of this point.

From the String Lake picnic area, there are at least two options for reaching the glacier. See General Approach (above).

Approach B. From the north end of Leigh Lake, hike around the west end of Bearpaw Lake and east end of Trapper Lake, then bushwhack north for another half mile or so to the drainage from the Skillet Glacier. Turn west and climb brushy moraine to the toe of the glacier. About 6.5 miles of hiking are required to reach the glacier from the String Lake·picnic area.

Approach C. Canoe across Leigh Lake to the gully that descends from the Falling Ice Glacier and hike to the saddle between the East Horn and Point 9808. Descend about 200 feet on the north side, then contour around the rugged east shoulder of the East Horn to the Skillet Glacier. About 1.7 miles of heavy duty hiking are required to reach the glacier plus the short portage between String Lake and Leigh Lake.

The Route. This is really simple compared to the approaches. Climb straight up the glacier to the bergschrund which is passed on the left by scrambling up an island of exposed rock; in early summer, these slabs may be covered with snow. Continue up the glacier and climb the steep upper couloir to a bifurcation at 12,160 feet. Take the left branch which tops out on the summit plateau.